JESUS'
URGENT MESSAGE
FOR TODAY

JESUS'
URGENT MESSAGE
FOR TODAY

The Kingdom of God in Mark's Gospel

ELLIOTT C. MALONEY, O.S.B.

continuum
NEW YORK · LONDON

Dedicated to four great scholars of Brazil:
Carlos Mesters, Johan Konings, Gilberto Gorgulho, and Ana Flora Anderson.
Their insights, along with their holiness and dedication, have opened up for
all the meaning of the Gospel of Mark and its urgent plea for today's world.

Cover design: Laurie Westhafer

Library of Congress Cataloging-in-Publication Data
Maloney, Elliott C.
    Jesus' urgent message for today : the kingdom of God in Mark's gospel
/ Elliott C. Maloney.
        p. cm.
    Includes bibliographical references and index.
    ISBN 0-8264-1604-7 (pbk.)
    1. Kingdom of God—Biblical teaching.   2. Bible. N.T. Mark—
Criticism, interpretation, etc.   I. Title.
BS2417.K5M295   2004
226.3'06—dc22

                                                                2003021666

Printed in the United States of America
        04 05 06 07 08 09   10 9 8 7 6 5 4 3 2 1

CONTENTS

PREFACE AND
ACKNOWLEDGMENTS

A few years ago I acted on a whim that changed my scholarly outlook and, to tell the truth, my whole life. Back in 1993, when some of the members of our Benedictine foundation in Brazil came here to Saint Vincent Archabbey to study, I became very interested in their country. The stories they told about home spoke of their deep faith and profound grasp of the meaning of the Bible for our Christian life today. I got it into my head to study their language, Portuguese, and to visit their priory in Vinhedo, a small city in Brazil near São Paulo. My abbot was delighted with the prospect and asked that I use the summer of 1994 to meet with the religious leaders who had gathered around the priory and its retreat center and work with them on the basics of modern Catholic critical interpretation of the Bible.

Giving those lectures and conducting the community retreat in Portuguese at the priory gave me a real workout over some seven weeks that summer (winter in Brazil), but I had a truly great experience. I was overwhelmed by the goodness of the Brazilian people and I knew I had to return some day. Little did I know that this scholar and seminary professor of some twenty years would return as a student!

The opportunity came when I took my sabbatical semester in Vinhedo in the spring of 1997. I wanted a change of venue from our busy scholastic scene and the seclusion and tranquility to write, of all things, some memories of growing up as a Catholic boy in the 1950s in Pittsburgh. My abbot gave me a task to do to earn my keep at the Vinhedo Priory, and that was to instruct the novices (the young men preparing to take monastic vows) in a critical appreciation of the Gospels. This I gladly did, since I had written my doctoral dissertation on the language of the Gospel of Mark and had been teaching the Synoptic Gospels for years. As I started to prepare my lessons, I remembered some of the awful gaffes I had made before in the language of

Brazil in my lectures of 1994 and so I thought it would be wise to read up on the subject of Gospel introduction in Portuguese, to get the technical language more properly in hand. Following the advice of our Fr. Leo Rothrauff at the priory, I selected some books on the Gospels by the Brazilian scholars Carlos Mesters and Gilberto Gorgulho, two well-known exegetes and teachers. I was astounded with what I read! These small books were the best Bible commentary I had read in years. As the awareness came over me that their kind of understanding of the context of the Gospels was far superior to anything I knew, I realized that I had to learn more about this exciting way of reading the Gospels. But by then my time on sabbatical had run out.

Upon my return to the States, I started planning to go back to Brazil right after the end of school the next spring to visit with some of the wonderful Bible scholars and to buy all the books I could. After procuring the necessary funding, I arranged to make a visit to Mexico City after the Brazil trip, since I had some great friends there as well. Upon my arrival in São Paulo I was lucky enough to meet and spend the day with Frey Gilberto Gorgulho and Dr. Ana Flora Anderson at the Dominican seminary there. I then made what turned out to be a pilgrimage to a small town called Angra dos Reis, near Rio de Janeiro, where I spent a wonderful day with Frey Carlos Mesters, whose ideas on New Testament eschatology took my breath away. The final scholarly interview took place on a two-day visit with the delightful P. Johan Konings at the Jesuit seminary in Belo Horizonte, just north of Rio de Janeiro in Brazil. Their library was particularly good, and the Jesuits made me feel quite at home. I returned to São Paulo, scoured the religious bookstores, and left Brazil with a suitcase full of books and periodicals. I ended this study trip in Mexico City, where I was not so lucky. By then the spring term had already ended and other duties took up the time of most of these busy scripture scholars. I was able, however, to use the excellent library of the diocesan seminary of Mexico City and to visit two other seminaries and a monastery in that part of the world, and so I was able to pick up some very good commentaries in the Spanish language.

As I read this material during the following school year, I discovered more authors and periodicals and made a decision to spend part of the next summer with the vast holdings of the library of the Pontifical Biblical Institute in Rome. Ah, the things one will do for scholarship! I had studied in Rome in the early 1970s and had taken a sabbatical semester there in 1990. I was delighted to return to visit the Eternal City and its excellent biblical library. On my return to the States later that summer, I shared my new discoveries with my seminar colleagues at the Catholic Biblical Association annual meeting. My ideas were well received and I experienced some good give-and-take in particular about the eschatological thrust of the Gospel of Mark. Later that year I was invited to participate in a panel on the Gospel of Mark at the annual meeting of the Society of Biblical Literature. Strong criticism, mixed with positive and interested response, greeted me at that convention in November 1999.

Having read all about this remarkable way of reading the biblical text, I knew it was time to actually read the Bible with the people in Latin America. With a very generous grant once again from the Brooks Institution, I set out in the summer of 2000 on a seven-week study trip to Mexico, Venezuela, and Brazil. On this memorable excursion I was able to visit seminaries, monasteries, and Bible study institutes; I met with several wonderful Bible study groups, with the Bible teachers themselves, group leaders, base communities, married couples, pastors, monks, and seminarians, and I even visited the leader of a community on possessed land.

In all of these refreshing encounters, I realized that I was actually experiencing the cultural differences that social science interpreters have been maintaining as absolutely necessary for a correct understanding of the ancient texts. The next logical step was to read up on the topic, and so I worked with my students here at Saint Vincent Seminary in several M.A. seminars on this approach to the Synoptic Gospels. Finally, it dawned on me that it would be an excellent idea to combine the theoretical knowledge of social science interpretation with the actual experience of reading the Bible with my Latin American friends in a discussion of a subject that mystifies so many, the eschatology of early Christianity. The result of this saga, then, is this book.

I want to thank my Benedictine community here at Saint Vincent Archabbey for the generous support I have received in this endeavor over the past five years, indeed, for all they have given me in the thirty-five years of my monastic life. Hearty thanks to the Brooks Institution for their generous funding of my 1998 and 2000 study tours in Brazil, Mexico, and Venezuela, where I was able to meet so many wonderful people who taught me so much. Without the help of these open and generous folks of Latin America I doubt that I would ever have come to the understanding that allowed me to write this book. To my students at Saint Vincent Seminary, whose excellent work especially in recent M.A. seminars has greatly expanded my ability to express this new approach, I owe a great debt for their insights as well as for their patience. I am also very grateful to my students at Saint Vincent College and to the many Christian believers who participate with me in adult Bible studies. Their feedback, as well as their great enthusiasm for the Sacred Scriptures, has made my study an easy and pleasant task.

INTRODUCTION

Christian believers often ask how God communicates to us the next steps in the eternal plan for the salvation of the world. How will the churches recognize the reforms needed to make ever more present God's will in our modern, complicated, and broken world? One very important means we have is to search the Sacred Scriptures over and over again and to listen for God's ongoing revelation. Not only do new questions call forth new solutions, but new ways of reading and rereading the ancient texts bring forth new insights for modern problems. One very meaningful development in NT study and interpretation presents some very powerful new possibilities for understanding Jesus' message in the Gospels. This is the realization that we need to read the text with a better comprehension of the ancient culture in which it was produced.

One part of the Gospel message, a teaching that has been largely neglected for many years, holds the promise of a truly renewed vigor for Christian leadership in our troubled world. This is the obscure and often poorly understood area of eschatology, or the Gospel's teaching on the future of the Kingdom of God that was the center of Jesus' teaching.

A couple of years ago, when everyone was excited about all the possible dangers and difficulties of the approach of the year 2000, there was a distinct rise in queries about the New Testament's teachings on Judgment Day and the Second Coming of Christ. Did Jesus really preach that the world was coming to an end? What are we supposed to believe about the millennium and other images in the Book of Revelation? What do the Gospels have to say about the "end of the world"? Does the theme of eschatological theology in the New Testament have any relevance for modern Christians? These are some of the questions that still puzzle us today, even though the turn of the millennium was to some disappointingly undramatic and is by now mostly forgotten.

THE PROBLEM

Most Americans are not quite sure what the concept "eschatology" means. A quick look at Webster's Dictionary tells us that the word derives from the Greek adjective for "last" *(eschatos),* and that its meaning is "the study or science dealing with the ultimate destiny or purpose of humankind and the world." In terms of the Bible, eschatology refers to the ultimate destiny or purpose of humanity in God's eternal will and includes a description of what God has in mind for the rest of time. Throughout the Bible, eschatological thinking varies from time to time and among different prophetic figures. The best-known type is apocalyptic eschatology, a theology in which God's final act of salvation will be a sudden revelation *(apocalypsis* in Greek) of power that will utterly destroy evil and reward the good.

In spite of a vague awareness of these terms, most Americans are quite puzzled by the apocalyptic texts of the New Testament. A variety of historical and other factors are responsible for our present state of forgetfulness, but it is clear that the once-central eschatological thinking of the early Church receives little consideration in our modern day-to-day lives. A few think that they threaten a fiery end of the world, but most take them to speak of some nebulous destructive action of God in a far-off future, if they even think about it at all.

Biblical scholars have often added to the anesthetization of the New Testament's great ethical demands by a kind of demythologization of apocalyptic literature that misses its point. Many think that the earliest Christians expected an imminent return of Jesus from heaven to bestow final judgment and salvation along the lines of a violent Jewish apocalypticism. These early believers were wrong, the theory goes, and the "delay" of the Parousia combined with a spirituality of individual perfection in the ever more westernized Church to lessen apocalyptic fervor and almost completely curtail its literary expression.[1] Thus many think that the only proper understanding for today of NT apocalyptic texts is as some kind of individualized moral response. They would interpret such texts as Jesus' Eschatological Discourse in the Gospel of Mark (chap. 13) as emphasizing only the salvific *kairos,* or "opportune time," of the *present* moment for the individual believer. The New Testament has, in this thinking, little or nothing to say about the future of the Church, much less about the destiny of the entire world.

In addition to this diminishment of biblical teaching, there is now a great debate raging among scholars about the eschatological teaching of the historical Jesus himself. On the one hand, many claim that Jesus never used apocalyptic language, since most of what they consider to be his authentic teaching is oriented to present living. A good number of North American scholars who study the "historical Jesus" hold this view. They feel that the early Christians, imbued with a Jewish apocalyptic perspective, were responsible for the creation of most of the eschatological sayings of Jesus. The problem with this position is that the earliest Christians clearly believed that during his earthly ministry Jesus himself predicted that he would come again, in his *parousia* as the heavenly Son of Man. As we shall see, many words and deeds of Jesus in the Gospel of Mark constitute a lively apocalyptic tradition intertwined with his most central teaching, the Kingdom of God, which nearly all scholars attribute to Jesus himself. Not only that, but the New Testament shows that a powerful apocalyptic expectation colored much of the early Church's moral teaching and ecclesiology. Could the followers of Jesus have so misinterpreted his teaching?

In contrast to this position, the majority of scholars claim that Jesus *was* an apocalyptic preacher, but many of them maintain that he was simply mistaken. This position is obviously very difficult for most Christians to accept, and it has serious consequences for today's understanding of the gospel. All this confusion in the study of NT eschatology has brought about an impasse in the scholarly pursuit of this most fruitful biblical teaching. The unfortunate result of these assumptions for the greater Church is the anesthetization of an important force in NT ethical teaching and the confirmation of a rugged individualism in personal piety that is simply unbiblical. Worst of all, the eschatological challenge to the present state of the world goes unheard.

The dilemma, we propose, results from the presuppositions of scholars on both sides of the debate. They misunderstand eschatology, and especially apocalyptic eschatological texts, because they are locked into a "hermeneutical circle" of their own modern, Nordic, First World presuppositions. These include 1) a literal approach to biblical symbolism that overlooks its metaphorical meaning—and thus misses its point; 2) a quantitative, future-oriented concept of time that misunderstands the force of apocalyptic with regard to the present; and 3) an individualism that regards biblical texts as creating a myth of personal security and well-being while not addressing the despair of a world that still languishes in dehumanized conditions.

THE BEGINNINGS OF A SOLUTION

It is not the intention of this book to resolve the Jesus Debate on eschatology, but with our study of Marcan eschatology in its ancient setting we hope to recapture some of the original Christian striving to cooperate with God's plan for the world. To do this, we shall examine the Gospel of Mark, specifically to discern the Evangelist's understanding of Christian discipleship as directed to the salvation of the whole world. This is Christianity's eschatological goal according to Mark: the fulfillment of God's plan in the arrival of the Kingdom announced by Jesus.

The first part of a solution to the debate on NT eschatology will come about with the admission by exegetes (academic Bible scholars) that they need to broaden their understanding of the ancient world. They are already doing this by listening to scholars from outside the traditional academic study of the Bible, men and women who can shed much light on the culture and thinking of the ancient world in which the Bible was produced. The social sciences, especially historical sociology and cultural anthropology, are now examining in great detail the lives and history of the common people of old. Equally important, however, are those Bible scholars who work in non–First World countries where they can experience the type of culture presupposed in the Bible in the everyday lives of the people they live with.

NEW DEVELOPMENTS IN BIBLICAL INTERPRETATION

A recent renaissance in the scholarly study of ancient Palestine in the first century has greatly expanded our understanding of the context in which Jesus lived and carried out his ministry. The reasons for this new viewpoint are two. First, recent scholars have gone outside the traditional focuses on biblical texts to seek from various social science perspectives a more refined understanding of just what society as a whole was like back then. Previously, most historical study had been limited to the major writings and the durable artifacts of antiquity, things produced by and for an elite section of the population who controlled their society and had little to do with the common people. Examining only these materials produced a rather one-sided picture of antiquity that tended to obscure some of the most important realities one needs to understand what was really going on in the ancient Mediterranean world.

The Social Location of Scholarship

There is no doubt that the perspective of the common man and woman of antiquity and a familiarity with the ordinary events of their lives were lacking in the presentation of the New Testament until fairly recently. Such a lacuna in perception was probably a factor of the social "location" of the most influential interpreters of the New Testament. Over the twenty Christian centuries, the most widely preached and read explanations of the sacred texts have been done by Christian *churchmen*. As such, these gifted communicators were mainly concerned with the relationship of the Bible to church doctrine, to the Christian belief system and its moral code. They read the biblical text with a kind of spiritualizing selectivity that was not much concerned with the practical social conditions behind the words and activities recorded in the ancient texts. In other words, their focus was trying to find out what the Bible revealed about how to live a Christian life in an idealized and fairly static medieval

Christian society. Gone was the powerful social upheaval that the first Christians caused. The stories of their lives and struggles were spiritualized, and political and economic factors were no longer taken into consideration. Finally, the powerful leaders of the Church who interpreted the Bible for the illiterate masses were basically unaware of their own limitations and their presuppositions about society. They remained relatively insulated in their social situation as members of the cultural elite of their day.[2]

Recent Approaches to Biblical Interpretation

The second step in this new perspective is the work of modern biblical scholars who are often from very different social standing than their predecessors. In the nineteenth and especially the twentieth centuries Bible study was broadened by a circle of scholars that went beyond the narrow confines of church leadership. Gradually, the prevailing opinions on most questions about the Bible were constructed by the leading *academic* writers. But these scholars were limited, too. They were mainly white, Euro-American, middle-class males, most of whom had not yet come to an understanding of how their own "social location" and their Nordic individualism helped to bias their understanding of biblical texts. In fact, they believed their opinions to be rather objective, since they were employing a rather "scientific" approach to the Bible.

Happily, this situation too has been left behind. The prominence in the latter decades of the twentieth century of a good number of highly trained women scholars, along with the broadening input of the social sciences, has opened up the field of Bible study to many new ideas and perspectives. In fact, it has even allowed an incipient awareness of the value of the different perspectives of Latin American and other "Two-Thirds World" exegetes. With their different sensitivities, these scholars have been able to perceive many factors operative in texts of the ancient world that the "mainline" scholars simply missed. We now have a much more realistic picture of the society in which Jesus lived and taught, and one that leads to some new conclusions about his life and ministry. Their insights and challenges for all Christians about NT eschatology and the present state of the world should no longer go unheard. The practical focus of Jesus' rejection of the formal religious system of the Jerusalem Temple, his teaching on justice, and his great vision for the future come more fully to light only when we read the Scriptures with a fuller awareness. The cultural understanding of first-century Mediterranean people, so similar to that in Latin America today, is a necessary ingredient for the veracity of any modern interpretation of the Bible.

No generation can say the ultimate word on the interpretation of any biblical text, but we have certainly come a long way in understanding the background and original intention of the writers of Scripture. There has been a reawakening of interest in Jesus' teaching on the future, and it has become the focus of many Latin American publications and Bible study groups. Through their insights and challenges we should be able to hear the message of Jesus speak loud and clear to the needs of our present world.

The Latin American Advantage

Over the past few decades Latin American exegetes have presented a more biblical understanding than have the majority of North Atlantic scholars in the three cultural areas mentioned above: symbolic thought, the perception of time, and the solidarity of humankind. Their insights can be too readily dismissed as "liberation theology," a generalization based on a caricature of some early efforts of Latin American theologians. In this book, however, we hope to show how the culture from which their recent study and publication have sprung is much closer than ours to that of Jesus and the early Church. Anyone who has traveled to Latin America has too many anecdotes about the difference in time perception there ("¡Mañana!"), and anyone who has been "taken" by a street vendor there understands that many Latinos have a rather different conception of social obligations and the rights and duties of individuals. These cultural differences of Latin Americans are actually quite a bit closer to the "Circum-Mediterranean" culture of the first-century Christians who lived in the Middle East, Greece, and Italy, those who started the church and wrote its constitutive documents.

Because of these similarities we have much to learn about the intentions of the original authors of the Gospels from Latin American Christians, who exhibit a remarkable consistency of thought whether it be in the scores of books and articles of trained exegetes I have read, or among the teachers and participants of the many Bible studies, conferences, and classes that I have attended in Brazil, Mexico, and Venezuela. These believers have a natural intuition that apocalyptic, with its symbolic mode of expression, is about people of every age and is focused on the potential for a just and peaceful life for all good people everywhere. They clearly perceive the duties of Christians in preaching the gospel to bring about a better life for all who would share in God's saving plan. The poor and marginalized of the world might not always be aware of all the literary nuances in a given text, but I have experienced again and again that their critical consciousness is powerful in evaluating both present society and an ancient text. In fact, their perspective has been called "the new hermeneutical key . . . that opens up or unveils the deeper meaning of many Biblical texts."[3] When they discuss a biblical story, they know they are discussing their own lives, and biblical history "becomes a symbol or a mirror of the present situation as the people experience it in their community."[4]

Their perception of the exploitation of the commoner in ancient Israel by the priestly aristocracy, along with their commitment to all members of society, reflects a cultural notion of solidarity born of a long history of suffering at the hands of political and religious oppressors. Finally, there is a significant difference between most Latin American exegetes and those of us who are North Atlantic Scripture scholars. In spite of immense teaching and pastoral duties, almost all of the former spend a great deal of time reading the Bible with the common people, people who are often marginalized and even illiterate. It will become obvious in the pages that follow that we have much to learn from our Latin American friends.

MYSTERIOUS MARK

The writer of the document we call "the Gospel according to Mark" is quite a mysterious figure. First of all, as any introduction to the critical study of the Gospels will explain, we cannot really be sure of the identity of the Evangelist and the circumstances under which the Gospel came into being. There simply is no reliable external evidence about who the author was, and the Gospel itself leaves its writer unnamed. For the sake of simplicity we will use the traditional identification "Mark" (and the corresponding masculine pronoun) when referring to the person who composed this the second canonical Gospel, while admitting that that writer's identity is still very much disputed. What the Gospel does tell us about "Mark" is that he was a very profound believer in Jesus Christ who wrote an impassioned narrative about the ministry of Jesus in order to manifest his message and true identity to a community in great turmoil. Mark urgently wants to show his readers that their suffering is according to God's plan, and that no matter how difficult it may be, their task of preaching the gospel is the only way to follow Jesus and inaugurate the Kingdom of God, the salvation of all who believe.

Second, this Evangelist uses an imperfect style of Greek when writing. We don't know if this is because his first language was Aramaic; he translated some of his source material literally from Aramaic into consequently unidiomatic Greek; he was trying to imitate the language of the Old Greek literal translations of the Old Testament (e.g., the Septuagint); and/or he was so bound to his Greek-language sources that he could only awkwardly incorporate them into his narrative. Perhaps all four of these factors are at times responsible for the rough style of the Greek text as we have it. Furthermore, scholarly efforts to distinguish Mark's own writing from the content of his sources have been remarkably unsuccessful except in very obvious introductions, conclusions, and transitions between stories. Yet, in spite of the unevenness of his style, more and more scholars recognize that Mark employs great skill and creativity when he chooses and weaves together the early church's traditions about Jesus to produce a fascinating and coherent narrative about the meaning of Jesus of Nazareth.

Third, Mark was very familiar with the Old Testament, and he uses it at times as a blueprint for the life of Jesus. Certainly many of the stories that he or his sources composed are full of allusion to OT texts, with the Book of Isaiah weighing in as the preferred prophetic voice. The text of Mark is so rich with possibilities of interpretation that we often cannot tell if the writer was consciously alluding to the Old Testament, or whether it was only sub-consciously present in his mind. Either way, of course, these OT allusions are extremely important for our understanding, as they were for Mark.

Fourth, Mark is very emphatic on the mysteriousness of Jesus' identity. In the whole first part of the Gospel no one has a clear idea of Jesus' identity except the readers who have been told in the Prologue that Jesus is the Messiah, Son of God, together with a couple of unclean spirits whom Jesus casts out of some unfortunates. Jesus refuses all notoriety and even tells some of those he cures not to mention the miracle to anyone. This literary feature of Mark is commonly referred to as the "Messianic Secret," but just what is being kept secret is debated.

Fifth, enigmatic Mark presents Jesus' central teaching, "the Kingdom of God," as a "mystery" that can best be illustrated by his parables, language that can only be understood by insiders. "To those outside everything comes in parables [= riddles]" (4:11). The outsiders, that is, the religious leaders who are the enemies of Jesus, are shown to have no understanding of who Jesus is. They are nonplussed by his indiscrete actions, while they are confounded again and again when they try to defeat him in argumentative confrontation.

Even with all of these difficulties, however, there is no need to despair of understanding what Mark is trying to tell us. After all, Christians have been reading the Gospel and have been inspired by it for centuries. We should maintain, however, a healthy respect for the mystery of this author who wrote over 1,900 years ago for an otherwise unknown Christian community whose culture was quite different from ours. There is undoubtedly a "sur-plus of meaning" in Mark's narrative; that is, we should expect to find more to this inspired work than was in the conscious mind of the author. It is a mine of Christian reflection organized by an author of profound faith in the power of God active in the life of Jesus and in that of all who follow him.

Mark's eschatology shows that although the final actions of God toward the world have begun in the life, death, and resurrection of Jesus, there is a definite future dimension in God's plan that involves the concerted action of Jesus' followers and his glorious return as the Son of Man.

THE PLAN OF THIS BOOK

In order to examine the eschatology of the Gospel of Mark we shall present this book in two parts. Part 1 will furnish the general information on the background and major teaching of the Gospel. These introductory steps are necessary for our more specific presentation in part 2, which will deal with the question of Mark's eschatology in particular. Thus in the first part, chapter 1 will present a working knowledge of the social history and cultural background of Jesus' homeland in the first century of the Common Era (C.E.). In chapter 2 we will discuss Mark's understanding of who Jesus Christ was ("Christology"). Chapter 3 will explore the central concept of Jesus' teaching, the Kingdom of God, as Mark presents it.

When we have completed our introduction to Mark's Gospel we shall turn in part 2 to focus on Mark's eschatology. Chapter 4 gives an introduction to the literary genres of eschatological writing in the first century and the understanding of symbol, time, and communality needed to comprehend it. Chapter 5 will deal with all the eschatological texts in the Gospel of Mark, excluding Mark's chapter 13, for which a detailed exegesis is provided in chapter 6. Finally, I shall present my conclusions on the eschatology of the Gospel of Mark.

In order to conserve space, I have not printed out the many references to the Old and New Testaments that form the background of our discussions. Thus it will be necessary for the reader to have a Bible at the ready and to take the time to look up and read the many passages we shall cite along the way. When I do quote Sacred Scripture, I use the New American Bible with its Revised New Testament, unless I have made a fresh translation to convey better the sense of the passage. This way, the reader can judge the helpfulness of this interpretation in every step along the way, hopefully to see the urgency of Jesus' gospel message for today.

NOTES

1. See David E. Aune, "The Significance of the Delay of the Parousia for Early Christianity," in *Current Issues in Biblical and Patristic Interpretation: Studies in Honor of Merrill C. Tenney* (ed. G. F. Hawthorne; Grand Rapids: Eerdmans, 1975), 107.

2. For more on this interesting subject see Marcus J. Borg, *Jesus in Contemporary Scholarship* (Valley Forge, Pa.: Trinity Press International, 1994), 97–101.

3. A. Nolan in the foreword to Carlos Mesters, *The Hope of the People Who Struggle: The Key to Reading the Apocalypse of St. John* (Athlone, South Africa: Theology Exchange Program, 1994), viii.

4. C. Mesters, *Defenseless Flower: A New Reading of the Bible* (Maryknoll, N.Y.: Orbis, 1989), 2. Mesters goes on to say that "by an unconscious intuition Latinos see the symbolic value of the facts narrated by the texts because they interpret the events of their own lives in exactly the same way" (ibid., 6).

PART I

The Background and Basic Theology
of the Gospel of Mark

–1–

THE SOCIETY AND CULTURE OF
FIRST-CENTURY PALESTINE

THE POLITICAL STRUCTURE OF
FIRST-CENTURY PALESTINE

It is widely known that Jesus of Nazareth grew up in Galilee, the northern part of Palestine, and that he was put to death in Jerusalem, the capital of the southern region, Judea. Most of us, however, do not know very much about the social and political reality of that part of the ancient Mediterranean world where Christianity began. That is because until recently even scholars have overlooked many elements of that region's culture. Now social historians and cultural anthropologists have brought to light remarkable differences between our societies, especially in how government worked, how the economy functioned, and the political nature of religion. Let us examine these differences in the areas most important for our study.[1]

The Government of the Roman Empire

The Roman Empire was made up of many small nations like Palestine, which it had gained by conquest in 63 B.C.E. Since it would have been impossible for Rome to supply the thousands of administrators needed for tight imperial control of all its huge territories, the emperor counted on the native aristocracy already in place in each country to maintain its colonial dominance. In such an "aristocratic empire," the emperor became the patron of these elite persons, who were put under the direct governance of the single ruler appointed by Rome. This Roman governor rewarded the aristocrats with large grants of land as well as high government posts in return for their support and tribute. Since wealth came from control of land and what it produced, the empire subscribed to a "proprietary theory of state," in which all the land, waterways, and any other resources were considered to be the property of the emperor. The task of the ruling class was to ensure that the lion's share of the profit of all that was produced was channeled to Rome and, in return for their cooperation, to themselves. They accomplished this by a system of extremely high taxation, upwards of 30 percent of the crop that the land produced. Sharecroppers were lucky to come away with a third of their crop because of extremely high land-rental fees. Of course, the peasants themselves had no say whatsoever in their taxation.

Ancient Imperial Economy

Palestine, like most of Rome's client-nations, was an "advanced agrarian society." In this type of culture about 90 percent of the population is engaged in farming and related occupations. The invention of the iron-tipped plow had made it possible for a farmer to produce a greater harvest than the farming family itself would consume, since the yield was now ten to fifteen times the amount of seed sown. Although today's farming techniques yield a much greater harvest (about fortyfold or more), members of the aristocracy were able to live off the surplus without doing much work themselves while enjoying the leisure required by "the noble life." It is estimated that it required the labor of ten peasants to support one aristocrat.[2]

Such a state of affairs was made possible by a myth of reciprocity in which, in exchange for the peasants' labor, the aristocracy supposedly provided protection from external enemies.[3] Second, by dictating the rules of production and regulating the transport and sale of goods, the aristocracy also supposedly guaranteed the prosperity of the land. In reality, there was little threat of an attack on places like Palestine, since in the first century most of the conflicts the Roman Empire engaged in were wars of conquest. The elite governing class simply used their dominance of the land to exploit the peasants in every possible way. When they did mandate any improvements in the infrastructure (roads, aqueducts, harbors, sewers), it was solely for the advantage of elites and their retainers, as was the construction of theaters, gymnasia, baths, and religious temples. The situation was the epitome of exploitation and "taxation without representation."

Because of their total control of domestic policy, the aristocrats in league with Rome created an "extractive" economy; that is, their conscious intention was to disempower the peasants completely so that the ruling class could gain almost the entire amount of wealth generated by the region.[4] They set the high taxes and tolls that the peasant farmers, fishers, and artisans were expected to pay. They controlled the courts where any disputes had to be settled, as well as the military that enforced all these decisions. It was impossible to address a grievance against the elites because they routinely "bought" any decision they wanted in the courts.

Social Stratification

ARISTOCRATS AND RETAINERS

The ruling class, that is, the ruler himself and his aristocratic minions, comprised only 1–2 percent of the population. It would have been totally unacceptable for these leisure seekers themselves to oversee the other 98 percent of the population themselves, and so they employed a large number of retainers (5% of the population) to do most of the work for them. The retainers acted as go-betweens, brokering the incredible power of the aristocrats to the lower class in a patron/client system most of us have witnessed only in movies about the Mafia. They were the tax and toll collectors, the educators, the military, the skilled artisans (who provided the nobles with luxury goods), the scribes (any of a variety of functionaries who could read and write), and the religious clergy. These middlemen derived their livelihood totally from their service to the aristocrats and were answerable only to them.

DISTRIBUTION OF WEALTH

All of these functionaries facilitated the high-handed dealings of the upper class and enriched themselves in the process by what has been called "honest graft," their "legal" cut of the surplus that the peasants produced in the land. It has been estimated that the tribute to the emperor, combined with the "take" of aristocrats and their henchmen, the retainers—together comprising only about 7 percent of the population—was about two-thirds of all that was produced. Only a third of what was produced was available for 93 percent of the people, a meager portion indeed.

POPULATION DISTRIBUTION

The lower class included the peasant farmers (about 80% of the population) along with another 3–7 percent who manufactured all that was necessary for farming (the artisans) or who did the menial and dangerous jobs, like mining or grave-digging. At the very bottom of the social pyramid there was what sociologists call the "expendable class," some 5–10 percent of the population who had nothing. They were homeless and itinerant, having been forced off their land by sickness or handicap, but mostly by debt. Many of these became bandits, lurking in solitary caves and attacking the rich caravans of goods being moved into the city strongholds of the wealthy. Others simply turned to begging for their sustenance.

THE PLIGHT OF THE PEASANT

In this tributary mode of production the high taxation led to the peasants' eventual loss of the land through debt and foreclosure. The elites controlled the prices of crops, and they could easily bankrupt a peasant by lending him money they knew he could never pay back. Farmers were reduced to share-cropping, where they got only a pitiable portion of what they grew, often on what was their own land! Land rent was high and the new landlords were able to control what was to be planted. Their greed resulted in orders to plant cash crops, like figs and dates, instead of staples, like wheat and barley, leaving very little for the peasant families to live on. They would now have to buy much of what they ate. Families often had to break up to find day-work. One thinks of the Vineyard Workers (Matt 20:1–16) who stood around all day in the marketplace of the nearest town, waiting to be hired by the steward of some landowner for whatever wage he was willing to pay. All this exploitation was seen as the normal course of things in ancient empires, and the peasants were utterly powerless to do anything about it.

One wonders how such an exploitative system could have existed for so long without rebellion. Aristocrats and their retainers worked in two ways to keep a lid on the situation. First was the constant reinforcement of the myth of reciprocity, that the aristocrats were the "great protectors" from external attack and the all-powerful providers of a successful economy. Second, the extractive economy left just enough for the peasants to keep them alive in this system of subsistence farming. Response to any resistance was brutality, meaning one lost what little one had, or faced imprisonment or worse. Think of the power of the (regional) king in the parable of the Unmerciful Servant, who "handed him over to the torturers until he should pay back the whole debt" (Matt 18:34). Loss of the breadwinner would surely mean starvation for one's family in a society whose bureaucracy was totally without concern for the welfare of the individual, and whose peasants had next to nothing to share with the poor.

The Political Nature of Religion

Another factor that guaranteed success to this abysmal system was religion, another aspect of society controlled by the elites. While private religious expression existed in the home, in ancient society everyone was compelled to participate in the public religion of the state. The public religion was universally seen as the chief means by which a nation pleased its gods, who in return for the sacred rites of prayer and sacrifice were believed to bestow fertility on the land and thus to allow the population to survive. All the religious functionaries, the priests who carried out the rites, the scribes who were educated to interpret the official doctrine of the religion, and even the menials who cleaned and maintained the temples, were supported by taxation just like other government officials. Their positions were therefore almost completely political, and their training and pay came as retainers for the aristocrats.

The priests were seen, of course, as the official teachers and functionaries of the religion, and they almost always reinforced the status quo dictated by the elites. Of notable exception were the great Hebrew prophets in OT times, but the institutional religion of Palestine with its priestly aristocracy and center of power in the Jerusalem Temple were all too typical an example of public religion throughout the Roman Empire. Jesus found them so scandalous that he acted out a powerful protest like the prophets of old when he overturned the moneychangers' tables in the Jerusalem Temple (Mark 11:15–19).

THE RELIGIOUS SYSTEM OF ANCIENT PALESTINE

Palestine under the Herods

When Rome set up the dynasty of the Herods as puppet kings of the new Roman province of Palestine in the first century B.C.E. the Hasmonean aristocracy was replaced with a new aristocracy of several priestly families invited to return from Diaspora Judaism outside of Palestine. These families became the elite clients of Herod the Great, who charged them to nominate the high priest, the chief official of the entire Temple religious system. With such status and its consequent political power they quickly took over control of the Sanhedrin, the religious supreme court, as well as the incredible wealth of the Temple's treasury. Now with vast economic power and the judiciary to back it up, the Temple's priestly aristocracy became the largest landholder in Palestine by foreclosing on mortgages they had given to overtaxed farmers.[5]

When Palestine was split up by Rome at the death of Herod the Great, the southern part, Judea, remained under the control of Herod's priestly aristocracy, whose allegiance was now to the Roman prefect. The Roman prefect, a type of governor, worked hand in hand with the Jerusalem aristocracy to extract the required taxes for Rome, while providing law enforcement for the decisions of the Sanhedrin, the highest religious judiciary in the land. Pontius Pilate was the prefect in Jesus' time.

The northern part of Palestine, Galilee, was ruled by Herod's son, the puppet king Herod Antipas, and his aristocratic retainers (the "Herodians" of the Gospels). The Temple aristocracy held less control there than in Judea. In both areas the traditional landed gentry joined these ruling elites in complete domination of most of the land and virtually all its production.

The Wealth of the Priests

The fabulous wealth of the Temple treasury has a rather ironic explanation. The Bible dictates that a tithe of 10 percent of everything produced each year in the land of Israel be given to the priestly tribe of Levites (Num 18:21) because they alone among the Twelve Tribes had been given no land since their Temple duties precluded farmwork. By the time of Jesus in the first century, the priestly aristocracy and their retainers, the scribes—their officials who were trained to read and write — had interpreted the biblical passage to mean that the priestly class could own land as long as they didn't farm it themselves. Thus the biblical idea was completely inverted: whereas in former times the priestly tribe (the Levites) was without possessions and had to be supported by the freewill offerings of the rest of the nation, now a fabulously wealthy priestly aristocracy was gaining even more wealth by their imposition of the tithe and other "religious taxes" on the impoverished majority of the faithful.

Religious Taxation

The priests and their scribes declared that the Bible mandated a tithe of all goods for the upkeep of the priests, and that God demanded a "head tax," a half shekel to be donated yearly for the daily sacrifices needed to keep the Temple pure. This latter sum was the equivalent of two days' pay for a day laborer with a good job. They further decreed that every year a family should spend another tenth of its annual income on pilgrimages to Jerusalem for the high feasts of Passover, Pentecost, and Tabernacles. Finally, a third tithe of one's income was to be given to the Temple every three years for the poor. There were also several obligatory sacrifices required of every Jew (explained below). So many sacrifices were held at the main altar of the Jerusalem Temple that it was continually in use, with tens or even hundreds of thousands of animals sacrificed every year.[6]

The Temple Sacrifices

The regulations for sacrifice to God in the Bible (Leviticus 1–7 and mentioned frequently in the Psalms and Prophets) were developed by the priestly aristocracy into an elaborate system of necessary tribute to God and purification for any and every infraction of the Law. They were seen as necessary for the restoration of the Jewish people after the Exile as exclusively the chosen ones of God. The daily whole burnt offering (holocaust) of one lamb in the morning and another in the evening was understood as an expression that God alone was the source of all the goods needed for life. Purity and reparation sacrifices were understood as a kind of purification of the Temple itself. These were seen as offerings to restore the desecration that was thought to ensue when individual sins dishonored God. So-called peace offerings were made to solemnize an oath and thank offerings were made to celebrate God's blessings of the past in reaffirmation of Israel's vocation as God's

Chosen People. While these latter two sacrifices were consumed by the faithful who offered them, the priests alone could eat the meat of the reparation sacrifices. Indeed, they ate so much meat that the Jewish Talmud says they were always sick from overindulgence. While the carcasses of the holocaust offerings were completely consumed by fire, the priests received the hides of the animals for their use.[7]

Emphasis on Holiness/Purity

Such an elaboration of the biblical instructions for the proper worship of God came about because of an emphasis on purity by the official interpreters of the Law. During the Babylonian Exile the Priestly Code was organized to keep the identity of Israel as God's Chosen People intact. At the return from the Exile, the priests were the native aristocrats who controlled the internal affairs of the Holy Land while under the foreign domination of the aristocratic empires of the Persians, of Alexander the Great, the Syrian Seleucids and, finally, the Romans. Their main strategy for the survival of their religion and thus their identity was to emphasize the "holiness code" in Leviticus (17–26). In it Israelites were to imitate the holiness of their God by remaining separate from everything that would defile that holiness: "Be holy, for I, the LORD, your God, am holy" (Lev 19:2).

This holiness was progressively seen as acquired and maintained by strict adherence to all biblical regulations on ritual purity. The scribes, the official interpreters of the Law (Torah), came to see their Law as one great instruction for the faithful Jew on the proper behavior to preserve purity. A special sect called "Pharisees" arose to guide the people forcefully to an exclusive renewal of their Jewish identity by means of a very strict adherence to this Purity Code. Their name means "the separated ones" because they separated themselves even from other Jews for fear of incurring ritual impurity.[8] The scribes, and especially the Pharisees, were obsessed with the polarities of clean and unclean, pure and defiled, righteous and sinner, in short, a whole identity as Jew versus Gentile. With this Purity Code they taught the faithful that whenever they incurred any impurity, whether physical or moral, they had brought upon themselves a terrible impairment to their well-being and to their status as Israelites.

In order to be cleansed of the impurity, relieved of its contagious nature, and forgiven for the infraction, one had to make a sin offering in the Temple and thus be restored to the normal state of the Chosen People. The great list of sacrifices in Leviticus 1–7 was consulted in order to bring about the reparation, but if one had not paid to the Temple all the prescribed tithes and taxes, one was in permanent violation of the cultic laws and could not avail oneself of the sacrificial system to make the offering and receive forgiveness. Catch 22!

THE REACTION OF JESUS

Jesus is presented in the Gospel of Mark as viewing the whole Temple system with its heavy emphasis on a purity interpretation of the Law as a travesty of God's will for his covenant people. This Purity Code separated the aristocratic priests (called "chief priests" in the Gospel) and those who brokered their immense religious authority, the scribes and Pharisees, from the common people. In effect the system marginalized the nonelites from their own social involvement in the community by proscribing any personal interaction with the "unclean," an almost unavoidable status given the number of regulations and the costs of the needed sacrifices for a return to purity. Furthermore, this exclusivity also completely eliminated any non-Jew from the worship of God and thus contradicted God's will for the salvation for all nations through the religious witness of Israel.

Jesus is never presented in the Gospel of Mark as criticizing the religion of the Old Testament. In fact, he is shown to be its greatest interpreter. What Jesus does, like the prophets of old before him, is to inveigh against the aristocratic practices of the Jerusalem elites, the priestly aristocracy, whose power base was the Temple and the Purity Code that they and their scribes insisted upon. He claims that the Pharisees and scribes "nullify the word of God in favor of your tradition that you have handed on" (Mark 7:13). What they insist upon as "the tradition of the elders" Jesus calls "human precepts" (citing Isa 29:13) and "human tradition" (7:7–8). Once again, to be absolutely clear, Mark's Jesus indicts not Judaism, but the small class of ruling elites who, as Marcus Borg puts it so well, "rather than representing 'the Jews,' are more accurately seen as the oppressors of the vast majority of the Jewish population of Palestine at the time of Jesus."[9]

Jesus' understanding of the Bible was completely the reverse of this kind of exclusivism. He affirmed God's *compassion* as the central teaching of the Old Testament and considered impure only that which was against the will of God.[10] His was a hope for an ideal state of social interaction based upon need, not wealth and power, in which all men and women were included. It seems that he upheld the Bible prescription of the remission of debt every seventh, or sabbatical, year and the restoration of a family's lost land at the Jubilee Year (the fiftieth year: seven times seven years according to Lev 25:10, 13–17, 23–28). The priestly aristocracy, however, had circumscribed God's intention with their interpretations and extensions in the oral laws that they had created. Two well-known instances of this deliberate circumvention of the Law of God were the *prosbul* contract and the *corban* system.

The *prosbul* (from the Greek for "application") provided for the contracting of debt without any hope of its being wiped out in the seventh or sabbatical year. This was ostensibly done in the name of mercy, to encourage unwilling lenders to lend to the poor with the secure hope that their loans would be paid back or restitution made. The *corban* (from the Hebrew for "offering") system allowed money to be consecrated to the Temple and its revenues to be used only for the tithes, taxes, and sacrifices of that institution, and not in any other way. This was a clever tactic if one wanted to avoid payment of just expenses, such as the upkeep of elderly parents (see Jesus' statement on this practice in Mark 7:9–13).

The Purity Code was self-effective because it mandated that all untithed produce was unclean and would thus pollute any of the faithful who partook of it. Worse still, the scribes and Pharisees made sure that people would not want to incur ritual impurity by insinuating that the purity/impurity distinction was synonymous with righteousness/sinfulness.[11] The poor were taught that when they could not pay the Temple taxes and sacrifices, they lacked God's blessing and should live in shame. This is probably Mark's point in the story of the Widow's Mite (Mark 12:41–44). Immediately after Jesus denounces the scribes who "devour the houses of widows" and who "will receive a very severe condemnation" (Mark 12:40), he points out how the widow is the victim of extortion. As she attempts to satisfy the Temple tax with two small coins, Jesus points out that "she, from her poverty, has contributed all she had, her whole livelihood" (12:44). There will be no welfare check at the end of the month. The widow is as good as dead.

On the other hand, the rich, who could afford to pay all their religious taxes and procure all the prescribed sacrifices, were therefore seen as favored by God. But again Jesus challenges the prevailing opinion. Ancient Palestine operated with a "zero-sum economy," that is, in a market system of "limited good." Unlike our modern economy, where money can be grown in investments and where the supply of goods responds to demand, "limited good" means that the quantity of all goods was assumed to be fixed. If one person got more of something, another was automatically being deprived. Thus rich people could grow wealthy only by defrauding their neighbors.[12] The rich got their power to do this only because they were either aristocrats or their retainers, and in Judea that meant that they got it from the Rome-backed priestly aristocracy or from the landed gentry in league with them. Full circle! The ones who dictated religious opinion were the ones who benefited from it most. The common people, like Jesus' disciples, accepted the notion that God must favor the rich because everyone said it was so. No wonder when Jesus said: "It is easier for a camel to pass through [the] eye of [a] needle than for one who is rich to enter the Kingdom of God," the disciples "were exceedingly astonished and said among themselves, 'Then who can be saved?'" (Mark 10:25–26).

We should keep in mind that the historical reality at the writing of Mark's Gospel was somewhat different than at the time of Jesus, for it was fully forty years later. The late 60s and early 70s of the first century were a time of great political upheaval, whether the Marcan community's location was in the Near East (Galilee or Syria), as many believe, at the end of the Jewish insurrection against Rome, or, as the majority of scholars hold, in Rome itself just after the persecution of Nero. The social location, however, was the same, for aristocratic agrarian imperial society was remarkably uniform throughout the whole Roman Empire. Thus the picture of society and culture we have drawn of ancient Palestine is valid for the understanding of Jesus in his own time as well as for Mark's portrait of him as the inaugurator of the community of the Kingdom of God. While Mark's vision is very much focused on the upheaval and persecution of his own time, he draws on the life and eschatological vision of Jesus which, he shows, predicted that all of it was to happen: "Be watchful! I have told it all to you beforehand" (Mark 13:23).

NOTES

1. In this chapter I am greatly indebted to the work of Marcus J. Borg, *Jesus in Contemporary Scholarship* (Valley Forge, Pa.: Trinity Press International, 1994), esp. chap. 5; K. C. Hanson and Douglas E. Oakman, *Palestine in the Time of Jesus: Social Structures and Social Conflicts* (Minneapolis: Fortress, 1998), esp. chaps. 3–4; William R. Herzog, *Jesus, Justice, and the Reign of God: A Ministry of Liberation* (Louisville, Ky.: Westminster John Knox, 2000), esp. chap. 5; Bruce Malina, *The Social Gospel of Jesus: The Kingdom of God in Mediterranean Perspective* (Minneapolis: Fortress, 2001), esp. chap. 2; and Anthony J. Saldarini, *Pharisees, Scribes, and Sadducees in Palestinian Society* (Grand Rapids, Mich.: Eerdmans, 1988), esp. chaps. 2–3. For those who read Spanish, Mexican scholar Carlos Bravo has good summaries of the social world of Jesus in his excellent book *Jesús, hombre en conflicto: El relato de Marcos en América Latina* (2nd ed.; Mexico City: Centro de Reflexión Teológica, 1996), 27–54 and 318–28.

2. Herzog, *Jesus, Justice, and the Reign of God*, 93.

3. For a fuller discussion of "false reciprocity" see ibid., 101–2, and, more generally on the patron/client relationship, see Saldarini, *Pharisees, Scribes, and Sadducees*, 56–59.

4. For a chapter-length presentation of the ancient imperial economy, see Hanson and Oakman, *Palestine in the Time of Jesus*, chap. 4.

5. For a fuller discussion of the Herodian aristocracy, see Herzog, *Jesus, Justice, and the Reign of God*, 90–92, and Hanson and Oakman, *Palestine in the Time of Jesus*, 82–86.

6. Hanson and Oakman, *Palestine in the Time of Jesus*, 143.

7. For a full description of the Temple tax and sacrifice system see ibid., chap. 5.

8. For further information on the scribes and Pharisees, see the excellent book-length discussion of Saldarini, *Pharisees, Scribes, and Sadducees*, esp. chap. 12, "The Place of the Pharisees in Jewish Society."

9. Borg, *Jesus in Contemporary Scholarship*, 105. William R. Herzog points out: "In chapter 7 [of Mark] attention shifts from the Temple to its 'constitution,' the Torah. Jesus did not abrogate the Torah or supersede it in his own teaching. Rather, he interpreted the Torah in

light of God's intent for it. The Torah was meant to be an expression of God's covenant with the people, a way of ensuring that God's land would be a haven of justice in an unjust world. This reading clashed with those who had co-opted the Torah for their own political interests" (*Jesus, Justice, and the Reign of God*, 109).

10. Johan Konings, *Marcos* (São Paulo: Loyola, 1994), 31.

11. This is also the conclusion of Jewish scholar Jacob Neusner in his *The Idea of Purity in Ancient Judaism* (Leiden: Brill, 1993), esp. the "Summary" on 118–19.

12. The ancient economic world was completely static; that is, there were no new lands, no new industries, no new farming techniques, and all commodities were limited and unchanging in quantity of production. Any new property, goods, or power had to be acquired at the expense of someone else. Thus those who amassed great fortunes could only have done it by some form of robbery or fraud in which they gained the rightful possessions of others. See the summary on "Rich, Poor, and Limited Good" in Bruce J. Malina and Richard L. Rohrbaugh, *Social-Science Commentary on the Synoptic Gospels* (2nd ed.; Minneapolis: Fortress, 2003), 400–401.

–2–
THE CHRISTOLOGY OF
THE GOSPEL OF MARK

INTRODUCTION

The Task of Christology

In order to have a firm understanding of the Church's belief in the person and mission of Jesus Christ, one must realize that the unfolding of divine revelation took some time to occur. Indeed, it is still going on for us today. The doctrinal formulations of the Church on Christology are the fruit of a long development of understanding that started with the public ministry of Jesus and grew clearer through the writing of the New Testament. The canonical Gospels, each of which is a special portrait of Jesus composed for a particular Christian community, are especially important witnesses of that growing comprehension in the first Christian century. The fine-tuning of Christian understanding, especially in the metaphysical thinking of Hellenistic categories of substance, nature, and person, was carried out over several centuries of reflection and debate.

From the fourth through the eighth centuries the Church held seven major councils to determine the basic points of Christian doctrine on Jesus Christ that we affirm in our creeds and catechisms to this day. In this light we can see that the Christological teaching of the Gospel of Mark is a truthful, but partial, revelation of the identity of Jesus Christ. But only by sticking closely to the text, trying not to read the Church's later understanding into it, can we truly comprehend the contribution of this Evangelist to the Church's full teaching on our Savior. Finally, I am not attempting here to give the Christology of Jesus himself, of the "historical Jesus," so much controverted these days. I think that I can make a contribution to that study only if I first do justice to the *Marcan* presentation of the identity and activity of Jesus Christ.

Recent Marcan Scholarship

In recent years the Christology of Mark's Gospel has come increasingly into focus as hinging on two key appellations of Jesus, "the Son of God" and "the Son of Man." The two titles are not opposed to each another, nor is one presented in order to correct the other. A second point generally agreed upon is that there is a decided secrecy motif surrounding the identity of Jesus, classically called "the Messianic Secret." But there is no complete agreement as to just what is being kept secret and why. Some scholars have tried to prove an errant Christology behind the title "Son of God," one that the Evangelist tries to correct. This effort has not borne much fruit, since the imagined false Christology remains a matter of speculation and there is no agreement on its specific character. A better way to see Mark's Christology is to examine what Mark has to say about Jesus as the narrative unfolds. This process reveals a tension throughout the entire Gospel in Jesus' identity that could only be resolved on the cross, and then fully understood in the ongoing leadership of his disciples by the Resurrected One in the new Church. I shall proceed, then, with a narrative Christology in which I examine the identity of Jesus as Mark unfolds it in the ongoing plot of the Gospel.

A NARRATIVE CHRISTOLOGY OF THE GOSPEL OF MARK

The Prologue of the Gospel (1:1–13)

The original title of the Gospel of Mark is its first verse, an incomplete sentence: "The beginning of the gospel of Jesus Christ [Messiah] (the Son of God)." The attribution to Mark ("According to Mark") came only later in Christian tradition and even later did its name, "the Gospel according to Mark." Thus the original author of the Gospel chose to entitle his narrative with an identification of its protagonist, Jesus. We know that Mark considers this description to be a correct (if partial) identification of Jesus because when asked by the High Priest if he is "the Messiah, the son of the Blessed One [= God]," Jesus himself answers with a resounding "I am" (14:61, 62).

MESSIAH

It is well known that the Jewish people at the time of Jesus were expecting a savior figure whom they called the "messiah," a Hebrew word meaning "the anointed one." This term is used in the Old Testament for various figures, but is mainly applied to the king, the earthly representative of God, whom the Israelites always considered to be the real ruler of Israel.

In the oracles of the exilic and postexilic prophets there arose the idea of a David *redivivus,* a coming king who would be an ideal ruler like King

David, who would restore his fallen dynasty in a new outpouring of divine power. In the entire Old Testament, however, such an expected figure is called by the name "messiah" only once, in Dan 9:25–26. It is only in the postbiblical Jewish texts just before and around the time of Jesus that the figure of an expected "messiah" becomes quite popular. Building on the OT hope for a David-like savior-king, the Jews came to expect a "Messiah" who would become the redeemer of Israel by his great power and awesome deeds to make their nation the center of a renewed world.

While Mark does identify Jesus as the awaited Messiah, that title evidently does not do justice to his role in God's plan since Mark sees the need to further clarify Jesus' messiahship by immediately adding a second title in his introduction, "Son of God." Moreover, when Peter correctly answers Jesus' question "Who do you say that I am?" in 8:29 with the response, "You are the Messiah," Jesus warns the disciples not to tell anyone about him. This is because the designation "Messiah" must be completed by the very next words from Jesus' mouth, when "he began to teach them that the Son of Man must suffer greatly . . . and be killed, and rise after three days" (8:31; repeated in 9:31 and 10:33–34). Jesus clearly questions the common expectation of the Messiah as the Son of David (= Jewish ruler with great temporal power) in 12:35–37, and even as he hangs dying on the cross the chief priests and scribes taunt him for not being the "messiah" they expected.

THE SON OF GOD

In the Hebrew and Aramaic languages of the Old Testament, the expression "son of X" was used to define an individual as participating in the sphere of, or belonging to, some readily identifiable person or group. For example, "the sons of the prophets" is a common appellation for a group of seers in the Old Testament. The expression "son of" can even denote the sharing of some quality, as Jesus calls James and John the "sons of thunder" in the Gospels. The wedding guests in Mark 2:19 are literally "the sons of the bridal chamber," and even an arrow may be called the "son of the quiver" in a poetic text (Lam 3:13). Thus the biblical appellation "a son of God" was used in the Old Testament for many figures to indicate the individual's close relationship with the power and dignity of God.[1] For example, angels are called sons of God in the Old Testament, as are prophets, Israel itself, the righteous person in Wis 2:13–18, and especially the kings of Israel.

In addition to all of this, in the Hellenistic world where Mark's readers lived (Mark wrote in the Greek language), some emperors and kings referred to themselves as "son of God," and the popular Stoic philosopher Epictetus called all virtuous human beings "sons of God." Thus to determine just what Mark means by "[the] Son of God" is difficult, and Mark never makes an abstract theological digression from his narrative to explain to us exactly what he means by any of his Christological titles. So it is best to start with the narrative of the Gospel itself, beginning with its Prologue, to see how the Evangelist begins to lead the reader/hearer to the Marcan understanding of who Jesus is.

In the very first passage of the Prologue (1:2–3), which is in fact a private disclosure to the reader, a combination of OT texts has been put together apparently from Exodus, Malachi, and Isaiah, but curiously referred to by Mark as what is "written in Isaiah the prophet." This fact leads one to suspect that Mark did not have copies of all the OT books in front of him but took over a *florilegium* (Latin "bouquet," meaning a selected collection of OT texts) from early Christian preaching. He recognized the last part of this early Christian tradition as being from Isaiah, the prophet most important to his presentation of Jesus, and simply attributed the whole quotation to Isaiah. Here are the three parts of this important introductory text in Mark 1:2–3:

> a. Behold, I am sending my messenger ahead of you;
> b. he will prepare your way.
> c. A voice of one crying out in the desert: "Prepare the way
>   of the Lord, make straight his paths."

Section *a* is from Exod 23:20, well known as an address to Israel in the desert, and so we may have here an identification of Jesus as a representative of God's people. Even more important, however, are the two textual changes made to the following OT texts cited. Section *b* is from Mal 3:1 where God is sending a messenger to prepare "my [= God's] way," but in Mark's citation of it the messenger is to prepare "your" way. In the context God's word addresses Jesus as the one whose way ("your way") will be prepared by John the Baptist (who is introduced in verse 4 which follows). Thus for Mark God's way has now become the way of Jesus. Section c, the last part of the catena, reads: "Prepare the way of the Lord, make straight *his* paths," where the paths "*for our God*" stands in Isa 40:3. The result is that in Mark's rendition of the text God is referring to Jesus with the divine epithet "Lord" and thus equates Jesus' ministry with the paths (= the plan) of God. Here then, at the very beginning of the Gospel, Mark identifies Jesus very closely with God, indicating that the "way" and the "paths" of his ministry are identical with God's design for the salvation of humankind, even while Jesus is also seen as the representative of God's people Israel.

After Jesus has been baptized by John, he has an empowering religious experience. The barrier between heaven and earth is torn open, the Spirit descends upon Jesus, and God's voice proclaims, "You are my beloved Son; with you I am well pleased" (Mark 1:11). Now the reader understands perfectly that Jesus is the Son of God. God has said so. But this divine affirmation, too, is filled with OT allusions. In Psalm 2, an ancient coronation liturgy, the newly blessed king of Israel says, "I will proclaim the decree of the LORD, / who said to me, 'You are my son; / today I am your father'" (v. 7). Thus we are presented with the idea that Jesus is the Son of God like the kings of Israel of old, the royal agents for God's work of salvation on earth.

It is, however, in the Genesis story of the Aqedah, the Sacrifice of Isaac (chap. 22), that the phrase "beloved son" occurs again and again. Here Mark's Christian tradition may be alluding to that OT sacrificial offering since Jesus' death was his supreme act as God's obedient Son. But the rest of God's statement in Mark 1:11 looks a lot like what God says in Isaiah 42:1, "Here is my servant whom I uphold, my chosen one with whom I am well pleased." This text gives us the key to the final part of Jesus' identity as Son of God in Mark's Gospel. The second part of the Book of Isaiah (chaps. 40–55) contains four elegant poems in which God speaks of a special Servant whose destiny is glorification through suffering for God's people. Mark here loosely quotes the first Servant poem (Isa 42:1) to foreshadow the suffering destiny of Jesus. Thus in the heavenly voice of 1:11 we are presented with Jesus as God's Son, the royal agent of God, whose upcoming suffering will be a sacrifice for the salvation of God's people.

John the Baptist has acquitted his task ("he will prepare your way") by admitting his unworthiness to announce "one mightier than I" (1:7). The theme of the "mighty one" is picked up by Jesus in the parable of the Strong Man (3:27) and refers to Jesus' absolute power over "the ruler of this world," Satan. In 1:8 the Baptist goes on to say that Jesus will baptize with the Holy Spirit. Immediately after Jesus receives this powerful gift of the Spirit, it drives him out into the desert to contend with and vanquish Satan (1:12–13). The reader can now understand why Jesus never has the slightest trouble in casting out any demon later in his ministry.

To sum up, then, Mark presents Jesus to the reader at the very beginning of the Gospel as Messiah, Son of God, the royal agent whose obedience to God will bring about salvation for God's people. We overhear God's voice to Jesus, calling him "Son," but also introducing the element of redeeming suffering and the sacrifice of a beloved son like Abraham, a theme reinforced as the Gospel unfolds.

This presentation of Jesus in the Prologue as the Son of God is confirmed throughout the rest of the Gospel, where we hear Jesus called Son (of God) seven more times. In 3:11 a report claims that again and again the demons recognized Jesus as the Son of God ("Son of the Most High God" in 5:7), evidently by their supernatural knowledge. By naming his inner identity they attempt magically to gain control over him and ward off his exorcizing power. In every case their efforts at neutralizing Jesus' authority over them fail utterly, and Jesus reduces them to silence, casting them out of the afflicted person. Their strategy had been to derail Jesus' saving work by identifying him as the royal agent of God of the popular expectation of the time. History shows that the common people of Palestine were all too eager to latch on to a popular messiah who would destroy Rome's imperial power and restore the Davidic monarchy to greatness. But Mark presents a God who will not use violence against the violent powers of this world. Rather, Jesus most reveals his heavenly Father and is most obviously the Son of God at the moment of his saving death, as the centurion proclaims in 15:39. Just the night before, Jesus had affirmed his identity as the Son of the Blessed One at the moment of his condemnation to death by the High Priest (14:61–64). God had reaffirmed this Sonship and proclaimed it to the disciples in the voice from heaven at the Transfiguration: "This is my beloved Son. Listen to him" (9:7). What Jesus says by both his words and his actions speaks the truth about God and God's plan for us all. Jesus is the Son in the parable of the Vineyard who will be killed by the wicked tenants, allegorical figures whom the chief priests, scribes, and elders recognized as referring to themselves, whom Mark says "were seeking to arrest" Jesus (12:12). Finally, Jesus calls himself "the Son" in the Eschatological Discourse (13:32), when he admits that only the Father knows the exact time of "that day."

The Christology of Part 1 of the Gospel

In the first part of his Gospel (1:14–8:26), the Evangelist portrays the beginning of Jesus' ministry in Galilee. As Jesus goes from town to town, Mark presents him as a tireless proclaimer of the Kingdom of God, a powerful wonder worker, and a wise teacher with great authority.

PROCLAIMER

As the Gospel begins, Jesus' foremost task is to proclaim the Kingdom of God. Mark's initial summary of Jesus' public ministry (1:14) introduces him as "proclaiming" the Kingdom. At the very beginning of his ministry, Jesus rejects the sudden popularity brought on by his success at healing. Specifically, he rejects Peter's invitation to capitalize on his spreading fame: "Everyone is looking for you!" (1:37). Rather, he insists on moving on to other villages, where his message is still unknown, "that I may preach there also. For this purpose have I come" (1:38). Throughout this first section of the Gospel Jesus goes about proclaiming the Kingdom by word and deed, in parable and controversy about the true nature of God's will.

I shall examine Jesus' message in the parables in the next chapter since they are in the main concerned with the Kingdom of God. It is in the Gospel's controversy stories, however, that Jesus' identity is most clearly made known. Mark has grouped his selections of these stories from the traditions about Jesus in several sections. In the first complex Mark has lined up five controversies (2:1–3:6). We find out here that the religious leadership in Galilee takes offense at every aspect of Jesus' ministry. First challenged are the scribes, who are probably the local synagogue leaders, then some Pharisees, the sect of strict enforcers of the Law and of "the traditions of the elders," Mark's code name for the Purity Code.

In these texts Jesus refers to himself twice as "the Son of Man," a title introduced in the text without preparation or explanation and, most remarkably, without reaction on the part of the listeners. "The Son of Man" reflects the heavenly figure of the Book of Daniel (7:13), who has "received dominion, glory, and kingship" from God in heaven. Since Mark saves his explanation of this important title until later in the narrative, we shall delay our discussion of it until we get to those texts. It is important to note, however, that already at the beginning of his ministry, Jesus can claim heavenly authority. He says that he has "authority to forgive sins on earth" (2:10), and that he is "lord even of the Sabbath" (2:28), domains reserved to God alone in the Jewish religion. Jesus' divine Sonship is no honorary title, but a (heavenly) reality that enables him to act directly to bring God's mercy to the needy. This author is the cause of the antagonistic relationship that the religious leaders immediately develop with Jesus, who does not heed their Purity Code when he eats with the common people and ignores their sabbath regulations.

After a brief interlude in which Mark shows Jesus proclaiming and healing amidst great crowds (3:7–19), we see the negative reaction of Jesus' own relatives and of some scribes from Jerusalem (who foreshadow Jesus' fate in that city). In response to the relatives who say that "he is out of his mind" (3:21), Jesus proclaims that his real mother and brothers and sisters are those who do God's will (3:35). To the scribes' accusation that he is possessed, he retorts that their logic is stupid (3:23–26). Moreover, to say that he is connected with Satan is nothing less than blasphemy against the Holy Spirit, which the reader knows Jesus has received after his baptism. The scribes have committed an unforgivable sin (3:29).

An important narrative for Jesus' identity is Mark's story at the beginning of chapter 6. While Jesus was teaching in the synagogue in his hometown of Nazareth, the people "took offense at him" because they couldn't understand where a neighbor of theirs could have received such wisdom. They say, "Is he not the carpenter, the son of Mary, and the brother of James and Joses and Judas and Simon?" (6:3). Jesus' response is quite interesting: "A prophet is not without honor except in his native place and among his own kin" (6:4). Here Mark tells us that in his ministry of proclaiming, Jesus considers himself to be a prophet, something that a lot of other people thought about Jesus (see 6:15 and 8:28). The prophets of the Old Testament were very well known to the people as the ones chosen by God to constantly challenge the leadership of God's people. Jesus then sends out the twelve disciples, whom he had specially appointed to "preach and to have authority to drive out demons" (3:14–15), to proclaim repentance (6:12), warning that they, too, will be very controversial in their ministry.

In a long dialogue (7:1–23), the Pharisees and some Jerusalem scribes confront Jesus on the question central to their whole Purity Code: clean and unclean food. Jesus answers them by chiding their perversion of God's law by their "traditions" and takes point-blank aim at them by declaring all foods clean (7:19). Thus Jesus has confounded all comers among the religious leadership in Galilee with his straightforward responses in which he presents, with unheard-of authority, God's point of view on matters central to the religious and social dimensions of Jewish life. He shows that the scribes and the Pharisees are very far from the truth of what God wants for the people of God's covenant.

WONDER-WORKER

Most important to Mark's identification of Jesus is his wonder-working activity, although it is almost entirely confined to the first part of the Gospel (chaps. 1–8). Jesus is presented as a wonder-worker who performs "powerful deeds and signs" of three kinds: healings, exorcisms, and what have been called "nature miracles." Mark records some ten healing miracles before Jesus arrives in Jerusalem in chapter 11. These miracles are a constant feature of Jesus' ministry and not something of which Mark is ashamed. Some interpreters of the Messianic Secret have claimed that Mark was forced by his traditions to incorporate the miracles into his Gospel but downplays them by having them identified as "teaching" or by Jesus' commands to silence on the matter. Indeed, Jesus does sometimes forbid those cured to proclaim what has happened, but he does it in order to protect against the false hopes of an earthly messiah so easily aroused in the crowds. As we have seen, Jesus has made clear his attitude on this kind of notoriety at the outset of his ministry (1:38). But the stories of Jesus' healing are essential for a correct understanding of who he is. They are, in fact, a central part of his "teaching" on the Kingdom.

In his healing ministry Jesus does not practice self-aggrandizement, but in every case he trusts God, often inviting the afflicted to have the same faith that he has in God's goodness and saving power. Jesus brings salvation to the sick and handicapped by inviting them back to their proper place in society. For example, his cures allow Peter's mother-in-law to tend to her household duties (1:31), the cured leper to go to the priest as prescribed by Law and so officially be restored to society (1:45), the former paralytic to return to his proper place at home (2:11–12), and so on. Jesus is doing God's work of restoring creation by returning those marginalized by the unjust regulations of the religious Purity Code. All of this underlines the main task of Jesus as Mark presents him: he proclaims to all willing people an equal and free participation in God's Kingdom.

It is important to observe how Mark and the early Christian tradition present Jesus in his healing ministry. Jesus walks with the common people; he listens to them and takes pity on them. To show the depth of Jesus' compassion, Mark uses a very strong word to show Jesus' emotion when confronted with the helplessness of those in need. When a leper begs Jesus to be rid of his marginalizing disease, and two times when the crowds that follow him are hungry, Mark uses the verb *splanchnizomai,* "be moved with compassion," to indicate Jesus' response to the situation. The root of this verb means the "viscera, the inner organs" of a human being, and so indicates a powerful emotional, even physical reaction. In several other stories Jesus stops what he is doing, overcome with the presence of injustice, as when the widow puts her last pennies into the Temple treasury, or the uncared for effects of disease or handicap, as in the cases of the Epileptic Boy (9:19) and the Blind Bartimaeus (10:47–49). Jesus is forcefully moved by the unfortunate because he, as God's Son, understands more than anyone the profound dignity of the human being as a creature of God, whose will is for the salvation and happiness of all.[2]

Jesus' power over the supernatural forces of evil has been shown already in the Prologue, but he continues a kind of "mopping up" operation as he goes along his way, destroying the essential reign of evil, without struggle, without a hint of failure. Several times the demon-possessed are shown to have some specific sickness, but Mark almost always calls the demons "unclean spirits." This is important because the truly dehumanizing feature of demon possession was understood to be that it rendered the afflicted persons ritually unclean and therefore cut them off from their normal societal life. Such marginalization for a first-century Jew was a complete negation of the meaningfulness of life. Jesus drives out the demons simply and effectively and the possessed are restored to their proper place in society, recreated, as it were, as full human beings once again or even for the first time. "Quiet! Come out of him" (1:25): with these words Jesus restores control of his life to the possessed man.

Jesus' "nature miracles," his stupendous feats of twice feeding a multitude with a few loaves of bread, of calming a storm at sea, and walking on water are all orchestrated to show that his power comes from God. They are presented in imagery very similar to that of God's powerful prophet Elisha (who miraculously feeds a hundred people in 2 Kings 4:42–44), and they imitate God's absolute dominance of the sea, that mythical symbol of chaos in the Old Testament (Ps 65:8; 106:9; Jonah 1:4). These "nature miracles" allow the disciples a glimpse of the final glorious destiny of the Son of God and his messianic banquet. Much as in the Transfiguration (9:2–8), the veil that camouflages the heavenly reality of the Son of God from earthly perception is turned back.

TEACHER

In addition to Mark's presentation of Jesus as proclaimer and wonder-worker in the first part of the Gospel, Jesus is also called "teacher" twice and his "teaching" mentioned some thirteen times. In the first mention of Jesus' teaching we see the Marcan habit of repeating what he wants to emphasize: Jesus "*taught* . . . [they] were astonished at his *teaching,* for he *taught* them as one having authority" (1:21, 22). Mark does not tell us the content of that teaching, but only that the audience was astonished when he cast out the unclean spirit. Then they say: "What is this? A new teaching with authority" (1:27). The second mention of Jesus' teaching (2:13) is also without record of what Jesus said, but the narrative tells of Jesus calling Levi the toll collector to follow him. These episodes show us that for Mark Jesus' teaching is not only in what he says but also in what he does. In the first story he frees a human being by casting out a demon (1:23–26), and in the second he reinstates a marginalized person to society and even asks him to be a follower, thus breaking down the barriers between clean and unclean (2:14). The fact that Jesus teaches about the Kingdom of God in his actions is confirmed later by Mark when he says that Jesus "teaches" that he "*must* suffer greatly . . . and be killed" (8:31; cf. 9:31). The Greek word *dei* ("must; it is necessary that") indicates God's will, that is, the true requirement of the Kingdom, also in 13:7, 10; 14:31.

A second round of teaching occurs in Jesus' parables in chapter 4, and in 4:33–34 Mark emphasizes by repetition that Jesus taught *only* in parables. The parables will be discussed in the next chapter, but we should note here that Mark's Jesus teaches that in order to understand the parables, one has to follow his example of a life of total dedication to God's will, whether in tribulation, persecution, or worldly anxiety (4:17–19).

The Christology of Part 2 of the Gospel

The turning point of the whole Gospel occurs at its middle in a scene at Caesarea Philippi. Here Jesus discloses his full identity to his disciples, namely that he, as the Messiah, Son of God, must suffer in order to complete God's task for him in order to fulfill his destiny as "the Son of Man." In reply to Jesus' question to the disciples, Peter volunteers the correct answer: "You are the Messiah" (8:29). The readers/hearers of the Gospel know that this is correct insofar as it goes, but we are surprised at Jesus' reaction when he orders them all to be silent on this matter. This is the drama that Mark uses to instruct us that the messiahship of Jesus is only part of his identity, and that even so messiahship must be understood in a new way. Jesus goes on to say that "the Son of Man must suffer greatly . . . and be killed, and rise after three days" (8:31). In this response we learn that Jesus can indeed be seen as the Messiah awaited by the Jewish people, but that he is the Messiah that God has intended and not the domineering hero the people were expecting.

When Peter objects to Jesus' announcement of his necessary suffering, Jesus strongly rebukes him, calls him a Satan, and says, "You are thinking not as God does, but as human beings do" (8:33). Jesus will not bring about the military and political violence that people expected for the victory of Israel. Rather, as the true Messiah of God, he will enact a sacrifice of himself for the salvation of, and as an example for, Israel. He will be the embodiment of the Suffering Servant spoken about in the Book of Isaiah, who "gives his life as an offering for sin, /. . . / through his suffering, my servant shall justify many, / . . . ; / and he shall take away the sins of many" (Isa 53:10–12). But the final piece of the puzzle of the identity of Jesus is this strange title, the Son of Man, for Jesus says that "the Son of Man must suffer greatly."

THE SON OF MAN

The title "the Son of Man" is the key to the full interpretation of Jesus by Mark as the Messiah, Son of God, the one whose sacrificial death inaugurates the Kingdom of God. This unique designation is used fourteen times in the Gospel of Mark, but only by Jesus himself, never by a disciple or anyone else. To understand its meaning we must again turn to ancient Jewish texts since the phrase, literally "the child of a human being," has no specific meaning in Greek outside of Judaism. As we have seen, "son of X" in the Semitic idiom denotes a close relationship to someone or some group. In the case of the phrase "son of man," in the Hebrew and Aramaic languages it is nothing more than a common expression for "a human being" or "someone."

Although the expression as a title, that is, "*the* Son of Man," does not occur in any pre-Christian text, Christians see a connection of this title of Jesus to a mysterious figure in chapter 7 of the Book of Daniel. In a vision that is full of terrible beasts that oppress God's people, there appears "one like a son of man" to rule not only Israel but every nation on earth. It is important to note that "a son of man" is not a title here in the (Aramaic) language of this part of Daniel, but merely the common way of talking about "someone, a human being." The text is making clear that a *human* figure, in contrast to the beasts mentioned earlier, comes "on the clouds of heaven" and "receives dominion, glory, and kingship" over all nations everlastingly (Dan 7:13). It is debated whether this glorious human figure is conceived of as some heavenly figure in its own right or is more or less a poetic image (corporate personality) for the sovereignty of Israel. In either case, the character *represents* God's people Israel, since in the heavenly explanation of the vision Daniel is told that, like the "son of man" figure, "the holy ones [= Israel] of the Most High shall receive the *kingship,* to possess it forever and ever" (Dan 7:18).

The title does turn up in a first-century Jewish writing, the Similitudes of Enoch. In this text a figure called "the Son of Man," also identified as "the Elect One," is said to have been created before time to be the eschatological judge at the end of time. An appendix to another of its visions identifies the Son of Man as the OT figure of Enoch who, having been assumed into heaven (see Gen 5:24), was transformed into the eschatological judge. In this writing we probably have an example of independent Jewish speculation on Dan 7:13 as promising a cosmic redeemer who goes beyond the expectations of a Davidic Messiah.

In another late first-century Jewish text, 4 Ezra, the prophet has a vision in which he sees "as it were a *man*" rising from the sea and riding on the clouds. This figure will reunite the scattered tribes of Israel and judge the wicked. Such material, scant as it is, helps to confirm that in some circles of Jewish theological speculation the mysterious figure of Dan 7:13 was being considered as a messiah-like redeemer. However, to gain a more specific understanding of what the early *Christian* community meant by the title "the Son of Man," we must look at the gospel tradition about "the Son of Man" prior to the Gospel of Mark.

Although the title is never found in the writings of St. Paul, it does turn up in sayings traditions that are common to Matthew and Luke but not found in Mark. These "Double Tradition" texts are widely held to have been copied independently by Matthew and Luke from an earlier collection of sayings of Jesus, which scholars commonly call the "Q Document." Here there are ten sayings in which the title "the Son of Man" clearly refers to Jesus in two contexts. In the first, the Son of Man is the One whose glorious coming is awaited at the End of the Age (Luke 12:8, 40; 17:22, 24, 26, 30 and Matthean parallels), a figure very much like that of Dan 7:13. But the title is also used as a self-designation for Jesus during his earthly ministry as God's selfless agent through whom religious outcasts are welcomed into God's covenant (Luke 7:34; 9:58; 11:30; 12:10 and Matthean parallels). To explain this second usage we may look to the Book of Ezekiel where God addresses the prophet over ninety times as "son of man." In it we see God's call to the prophet in all his human weakness in contrast to God's omnipotence, and yet God mandates this human prophet to preach a message of judgment and salvation that will be rejected by his hearers. Thus the glorious "Son of Man" to come is identified in the Q Document as the same Jesus, the humble human being charged by God to gather all believers into God's new covenant.

When we turn to the Gospel of Mark, we find fourteen statements in which the title "the Son of Man" occurs. Seven of them fall into the two categories used in the Q Document, but there is a third Marcan usage in which the suffering and death of the Son of Man are mentioned. Thus in Mark there are three kinds of "Son of Man" statements, those referring to Jesus' present activity, his resurrection and glorious return thereafter, and his suffering and death. Mark uses the title "the Son of Man" in the first category only two times, and both are in part 1 of the Gospel. In these texts Jesus' identification with the heavenly figure of Daniel's "one like a son of man" presents the reader with the typical apocalyptic vision of divine power working in both the heavenly and earthly spheres of history. Jesus, as the Son of Man, "has authority to forgive sins *on earth*" (2:10) and "is lord even of the sabbath" (2:28), both divine prerogatives because he has received from God already at the very beginning of his ministry the "dominion, glory, and kingship" (Dan 7:14).

This glory was usually veiled during the public ministry of Jesus, but its full manifestation is the subject of three Son of Man sayings of the second category. These are similar to those of the Q Document, in which Jesus predicts that he will return as the Son of Man in his Father's glory with the holy angels (8:38; 13:26; 14:62). In the fourth of these "future" sayings, Jesus warns the disciples after the Transfiguration not to tell anyone of his heavenly glory that they had just witnessed until after "the Son of Man had risen from the dead" (9:9). This means that until after his upcoming suffering, death, and resurrection, his Transfiguration glory could only be misunderstood, as in fact it was by Peter (9:5–6). Here, then, is the link to the third and most frequent use of the title "the Son of Man" in Mark and the Evangelist's own special emphasis in eight uses of it. Jesus is most clearly the Son of Man in his passion and death (8:31; 9:12, 31; 10:33, 45; 14:21a, 21b, 41) because it is here that he most forcefully demonstrates the power and glory and kingship he received from his Father. In this unexpected paradox we shall see Jesus' incredible power to remain humble and trustful in God despite God's self-concealment in the most frightful menace to human life, death itself.

JESUS' TEACHING IN PART 2 OF THE GOSPEL

In this short part 2 of the Gospel (8:27–10:52) Jesus intensifies his teaching, at first to his inner group of disciples, the Twelve (8:34–38; 9:28–50; also 10:35–45). The message of this teaching is how to follow Jesus, that is, how to be his disciple by taking up one's own cross (8:34), how to overcome the power of demons (9:29), and how to be "the servant of all" (9:35). He then turns to teach great crowds on both sides of the Jordan River (10:1–31). But here the content of this teaching is the concerns of an ongoing church community: marriage and divorce, the childlike attitude required of all its members, and the evil of attachment to wealth. This change of audience from the inner group is surely Mark's hint that Jesus proclaimed the Kingdom not only to the disciples of his own day but also to the Christian believers for whom the Gospel was written, the members of Mark's struggling church. Christologically, then, we may say with R. Schnackenburg that "the Jesus who teaches the people of his time turns seamlessly into the Christ who speaks to the church."[3] Finally, and in the third part of the Gospel, Mark emphasizes Jesus' "teaching" in the Temple (11:17, 18; 12:14, 35, 38). Here the authority of all its religious leaders is contradicted by Jesus' absolute "authority" (11:28, 29, 33) from God to teach on God's kingdom and declare who is close to it, like the insightful scribe in 12:34, and who is not, like the skeptical Sadducees in 12:24.

The Christology of Part 3 of the Gospel

JESUS AND THE TEMPLE RELIGION

The final part of the Gospel begins with Jesus' entry into Jerusalem, seated on a donkey colt, so obviously alluding to the entrance into Jerusalem of the peaceful king and "savior" of Zech 9:9. The crowd is wrong in thinking of "the kingdom of our father David" (11:10) since Jesus has taught very differently about the Kingdom of God. Jesus accepts neither their nationalistic ideas nor the exclusivity of the Temple religion as corresponding to God's plan for all nations.

After cleansing the Temple of its exploitative commercial activity, Jesus is questioned by every group of religious leaders who draw their strength from its institutional religion. They challenge Jesus' authority to reform and his competency to interpret God's Law, the Torah. Ironically, this final demonstration of Jesus' teaching authority takes place in the Temple (11:27–12:40), the very site his absolute authority will replace, in a final showdown in which he vanquishes all who come against him, confounding them at every point. He says that the chief priests, the scribes, and the elders (who make up the Sanhedrin, the assembly that will condemn him to death) deserve no answer because of their insincerity. Moreover, Mark tells us that they themselves recognize that Jesus has made it clear that *they* are the Wicked Tenants (12:1–12) who will kill the "beloved son" of God, the Owner of the Vineyard. In the conclusion of the parable the Owner "will come, put the tenants to death, and give the vineyard to others."

Next, the Pharisees and Herodians are confounded in their attempt to ensnare him, and the Sadducees are silenced because they do "not know the scriptures or the power of God" (12:24). In spite of one well-meaning member, Jesus condemns the whole caste of scribes for their ignorance about the Messiah, their hypocrisy, and their exploitation of the poor in the name of religion (12:28–44).

In all of these controversies we see that Jesus confronts the reigning religious powers without looking for power himself, for in his confidence in

God his freedom is complete. With unprecedented authority, he unmasks the false "righteousness" of the religious elites, showing that their Purity Code does not express the holiness of God. All that official observance only oppresses and marginalizes the many, while in reality the mercy of God is near to all those who suffer. In a honor/shame society, Jesus' freedom and modesty as he gains more and more honor in each confrontation are too much for the religious leaders. They cannot afford to be shamed any more in their public exchange with him, and so "no one dared to ask him any more questions" (12:34). They must now resort to the only weapons left to them: treachery and violence (14:1–2).

THE ESCHATOLOGICAL DISCOURSE

In chap. 13 Jesus leaves the Temple area and gives an intimate group of disciples instructions on the future of the Temple and the coming tribulation. In this discourse Jesus predicts that many false messiahs will come in his name, but that Christians should never be fooled by them. When Jesus comes as the Son of Man in eschatological splendor there will be no mistaking it.

THE LAST SUPPER

Mark tells us that at Passover time the priestly aristocracy who controlled the Temple and their minions, the scribes, conspired by treachery to arrest Jesus and have him put to death (14:1). While Jesus is eating the Passover supper, his Last Supper, with his disciples he offers a blessing over some unleavened bread and a cup of wine, saying that they are his body and blood (14:22–24). When he qualifies his word over the wine, saying, "This is my blood of the covenant," (14:24) he alludes directly to Moses' ratification of the Old Testament, the Sinai Covenant. Moses does this by sprinkling the blood of the sacrificial lamb upon the people with the words, "This is the blood of the covenant which the LORD has made with you" (Exod 24:8). By his words at this Passover festival of the old covenant, Jesus signifies that the upcoming sacrifice of his body and blood will ratify the new covenant promised by the prophets of old (see Hos 2:20; Jer 31:31–34; Ezek 16:60). When Jesus goes on to say over the wine that his blood "shall be shed *for many*," (14:24) he alludes to the Suffering Servant song in Isa 53:11–12, as he did earlier when he said, "The Son of Man did not come to be served but to serve and to give his life as a ransom *for many*" (10:45). Thus, at the Last Supper, Jesus proclaims the meaning of his upcoming death as a sacrifice, a ransom predicted in the Old Testament, which applies to all who would join the new covenant.

THE PASSION NARRATIVE

In the narrative of the arrest, passion, and death of Jesus we have the culmination of Mark's identification of Jesus. Jesus not only knows that he must suffer and die, but he understands that he will be handed over to his enemies by Judas, one of his hand-picked disciples, and denied by Peter, another of them. In fact, by quoting the prophet Zechariah, he predicts that they will all run away when their faith is shaken: "I will strike the shepherd, / and the sheep will be dispersed" (Zech 13:7, quoted in Mark 14:27). The failure of his inner circle—Peter, James and John—to keep watch with him as he prays in "a place named Gethsemane" only confirms that he will face his ignominious death alone. Mark tells us of Jesus' confrontation with his own human frailty when he tries to share with the disciples his intense sorrow at what was going to happen to him, "My soul is sorrowful even to death" (14:34). Three times he prays to God and begs to be spared from his fate. But then, greatly strengthened by his intimate prayer with "Abba," his "Father," he is ready "to be handed over to sinners" (14:41). Jesus' revolutionary experience of God as loving Father gives him new eyes to evaluate the reality of his situation, and so with great dignity he announces his betrayal as the Son of Man and steps forward to meet it.[4] He receives Judas's kiss, reprimands the crowd for its violence, and calmly points out that his fate is the fulfillment of the Scriptures (14:49) as the disciples flee in panic, one of them literally running out of his clothes to get away (14:52).

It is before the Sanhedrin, that supreme court of the Temple religion, that Jesus brings about his own condemnation after his silence declares that they have no case against him. With tremendous irony the High Priest demands an answer to the very identification of Jesus that Mark has given us in the first verse of the Gospel: "Are you the Messiah, the son of [God] the Blessed One?" (14:61). Jesus responds with God's own self-identification to Moses at the burning bush, "I am!" (Exod 3:14), and adds the final part of his identity when he predicts, "And you will see the Son of Man seated at the right hand of the Power" (14:62). This absolute claim to divine Sonship enrages the High Priest and the rest of the Sanhedrin, all of whom condemn him as "deserving to die" for such "blasphemy" (14:64).

In the Passion narratives that follow, Mark shows how Jesus was mocked, tortured, and put to death just as the Suffering Righteous One described in the Book of Wisdom (2:12–22), another OT model of utter confidence in God. He is handed over to Pilate to be condemned and executed as a messianic pretender, a false "king of the Jews," the Roman way of saying "Jewish Messiah." The soldiers confirm this judgment when, as they torture him with shouts and blows, they mockingly salute him: "Hail, king of the Jews!" (15:18). They lead him out to be crucified in a parade of human cruelty where he is mocked again, this time by the priestly aristocrats and their minions, the scribes: "Let the Messiah, the King of Israel, come down now from the cross that we may see and believe" (15:32). But the death of Jesus stands this judgment of Roman and Temple justice on its head!

After vocalizing his feelings of abandonment on the cross by praying Ps 22:2 ("My God, my God, why have you abandoned me?"), Jesus gives a loud cry before he breathes his last (15:37). He expresses his exasperation at his oppressors' human conceit in their complete misunderstanding of God's plan and dies with a shout, not a whimper. Mark signals us that Jesus' death is not a defeat but a victory for God when the centurion declares, "Truly this man was the Son of God" (15:39).

In his death for others Jesus manifests perfectly the vulnerability by which God remains loving and trustful of humanity even at its worst. In his apparent weakness on the cross, Jesus is the "Stronger One" who overcame forever the oppressing and alienating power of Satan (3:27; cf. 1:7). This, too, is Jesus' program for all who would follow him, for all of whom "the Son of Man will [not] be ashamed . . . when he comes in his Father's glory with the holy angels" (8:38). It is for this reason that some of the ancient Fathers of the Church interpreted the appellation "the Son of Man" to designate Jesus as the representative of humanity. They saw him as the ideal human being who lived and died in conflict and suffering, completely free and faithful to God, his loving Father, who would not abandon him in the end.

Jesus' brutal death on the cross is the key to his identity and to his saving work. He is the obedient Son of God because his love is the same as God's love. It is offered, fragile and vulnerable, for the free acceptance or refusal of all human beings, be they saint or sinner. The holiness of the God of Jesus is not some sacral distance between the "pure" and the "impure," but a suffering presence of love that is greater than any violent force. God's self-concealment at Calvary allows the power of Jesus' filial obedience and trust in God to manifest itself fully. In the death of the Son, says Carlos Bravo, "God is revealed in an inverse theophany . . . as a suffering silence which denounces our [human] irresponsible absence when confronted with violence against life."[5] The losers were the crucifiers, not the crucified, for all oppressive power is against God's will, and humans can never supplant what God wants. Jesus had predicted at the Last Supper (14:24) that his death would be the bloody sacrifice that ratifies the promised new covenant with God of all humankind. In it they may identify their very lifeblood with that of Jesus in total acceptance of God's will in their lives.

But the silence of Jesus' death is not God's last word. When God raises Jesus from the dead, we see God's most effective plan for the redemption of human life. For all of us, "who perseveres to the end will be saved" (13:13) by God's power in our own resurrection.

RESURRECTION

Interestingly, there are no resurrection appearance stories in the original Gospel of Mark, which ends at 16:8.[6] The actual event of Jesus' resurrection, which Mark tells us he predicted four times, is indicated to the readers by the figure of a "young man," who mysteriously appears to the women at the empty tomb on Easter morning. His enigmatic words about Jesus are: "He has been raised; he is not here.... He is going before you to Galilee" (16:6–7). Mark gives no clarification of this pronouncement, and the women run away in fear. (What Jesus will do after his resurrection and the reason for the women's great fear will be discussed in the next chapter.)

CONCLUSION

To summarize the Christology of Mark's Gospel is very difficult since almost the entire narrative focuses on Jesus' identity. In the Prologue Mark gives the reader the inside information that Jesus is the Messiah awaited in Israel and announced by John the Baptist. In a clarifying scene there, we have a rare appearance of the divine presence to guarantee God's love for his Son. As God's royal agent Jesus will conquer the evil power of Satan that alienates people from their own society and from their trust in God. In the first part of the Gospel, Jesus preaches God's Kingdom, the state of being in the power and freedom of God that all humans are called to, be they sinner or teacher of the Law. His miracles provoke questions and wonder, and his dialogue with the religious leaders begins to overturn the deathhold of the religious exclusivity of the Purity Code, as Jesus welcomes all into the Kingdom.

In part 2 of the Gospel Jesus announces that his disciples (and the church) must follow his path of service and suffering in order to form a new Temple of God that will be "a house of prayer for all peoples" (11:17). Jesus is at once the unique Son of God with God's power and authority to announce and bring about the Kingdom of God, and God's Suffering Servant by whose passion and death believers are released from the power of Satan and brought into the new covenant. At the same time he is the suffering Son of Man, the ideal representative of all of humanity who must overcome evil solely by their confidence in God. In the Transfiguration God presented Jesus as embodying God's total revelation, when the heavenly voice says: "This is my beloved Son. Listen to him" (9:7). The Son of God goes alone to his passion and death and lives out the will of God as the Son of Man, the perfect representative of humanity, the paradigm for our noble calling to a new covenant with God, our loving Father. This is God's way, this is the Kingdom of God which all may enter now. God raised Jesus from the dead to vindicate his life for others and to raise him to his place of leadership of the Church into a future Kingdom that began in power with his death and resurrection. It is to this central concept of Jesus' proclamation, the Kingdom of God, that we now must turn.

NOTES

1. For absolute clarity, we quote in full the late Catholic biblical scholar and member of the Pontifical Biblical Commission, Raymond E. Brown: "To prevent confusion, it is well to remind ourselves that calling someone 'son' in relation to God is ambiguous. It need not mean divine filiation in the proper sense of having one's origin from God so that one has God's own nature, but may connote only a special relationship to God" (*An Introduction to New Testament Christology* [New York: Paulist, 1994], 80). This, of course, does not deny anything about the divine identity of Jesus Christ, but allows us to trace the development of that understanding in a sure and historical way.

2. João Luiz Correia Júnior, "A pedagogía da missão," *EstBib* 64 (1999): 67.

3. Rudolf Schnackenburg, *Jesus in the Gospels: A Biblical Christology* (Louisville, Ky.: Westminster John Knox, 1995), 24.

4. I have learned this and many other penetrating insights into the Gospel of Mark from Carlos Mesters. On Jesus' experience of God as Father see *Caminhamos ná estrada de Jesus: o evangelho de Marcos* (National Conference of Brazilian Bishops; São Paulo: Paulinas, 1996), 117.

5. See Carlos Bravo's revealing words on the portrait of God the Father in Mark in *Jesús, hombre en conflicto*, 298–300.

6. Note: The Longer (canonical) Ending of Mark (16:9–20) in our Bibles has some traditions about the risen Jesus appearing, probably the reflection of a later writer on Luke 24 and John 20. The abruptness of the original ending at 16:8 is usually cited as the reason for the later attempts in the church to conclude Mark's narrative, and these give rise to three different attempts in the manuscript tradition to give the Gospel an ending.

—3—

THE KINGDOM OF GOD

Nearly everyone agrees that the central teaching of Jesus in the Gospel of Mark is the Kingdom of God, but we North Atlantic scholars seem to lack the categories to properly describe it. Aloysius Ambroczic stated the main problem in his classic study of the concept: it is "a kingdom yet to come which is, paradoxically, already present."[1] A vast array of scholars have wrestled with this temporal question of the Kingdom's arrival, whether it is present or future, but far fewer have been able to articulate just what it is that Mark understood the concept itself to convey. So, rather than starting with the temporal nature of the Kingdom, we shall begin by laying out just what the Evangelist says about "the Kingdom of God," as he interpreted the traditions about the life of Jesus that were at his command. Only after examining the Gospel narrative in this way can we comment on the temporal dimension of the Kingdom of God, keeping in mind that the final word on Mark's eschatological timeline will be given in the last part of this book.

MARK'S DESCRIPTION
OF THE KINGDOM OF GOD

Mark portrays Jesus as announcing the Kingdom in his words and in his deeds, predominantly in part 1 of the Gospel (1:14–8:26), especially in its parable chapter (chap. 4). In part 2 of the Gospel (8:27–10:52), Jesus gives special instructions to his disciples, including four sayings about the Kingdom. Finally, Jesus mentions the Kingdom three more times in the

Passion Narrative (part 3 of the Gospel). Let us examine the image of "the Kingdom of God" especially in these passages.[2]

The Kingdom of God in Part 1 of the Gospel (1:14–8:26)

In this first main division of the body of the Gospel, side by side with Mark's development of the Messianic Secret, Jesus proclaims a new reality, "the Kingdom of God." The Greek word traditionally translated as "kingdom" *(basileia)* reflects the OT abstract idea of the dominion or rule of a king, where it is often translated as the "kingship" or "reign" of a certain king. In many texts God is seen to be the real king over Israel and over the whole world, but the actual phrase "the kingdom of God" turns up only in a very few OT texts, along with the equivalent phrase "his/your/my [= God's] kingdom."[3] In these texts the kingdom is the future, saving rule of God. It "expresses an eschatological hope for a period when God's salvation would be realized, when his dominion over the minds and lives of human beings would be accomplished, and they would be withdrawn from subjection to danger, evil, and sin."[4]

MARK'S INTRODUCTION TO JESUS' PUBLIC MINISTRY (1:14–15)

After Mark's Prologue informs the reader that Jesus is the true Messiah, Son of God, he introduces the public ministry of Jesus with a summary of its content in 1:14–15. He contrasts Jesus to John the Baptist by noting that Jesus only began his ministry after John had been taken off the scene, having been arrested and, as we find out later, put in prison by King Herod Antipas. Whereas John's message was "repentance for the forgiveness of sins" (1:4), Jesus proclaims "the gospel of God" (1:14). The Greek word for "gospel" *(euangelion)* echoes the OT idea of the announcement of the "good news" of salvation for Israel (2 Sam 18:20–27; 2 Kings 7:9; Isa 40:9; 41:27; 52:7), a concept made famous in the early Church by St. Paul some twenty years before Mark wrote his Gospel. For Paul, the "gospel of God" meant the content of Christian preaching about Jesus Christ, "the good news that has its origin in God,"[5] which Paul calls "the power of God for the salvation of everyone who believes" (Rom 1:16; cf. 16:25). Mark confirms for us that this same gospel, known and believed in by the early Church, was the very center of Jesus' proclamation during his public ministry. That is why we can translate the very first verse of Mark's story "the beginning of the gospel *proclaimed* by Jesus Christ, the Son of God," as well as "the beginning of the gospel *about* Jesus Christ, the Son of God" (1:1).

But there is another aspect to the Greek word for "good news." In the Roman Empire "gospel" was commonly used in the emperor cult to mean the announcement of the accession of a new emperor to the throne. Thus St.

Paul and the early Church's preaching implied that what Jesus announced was nothing less than the ascendancy of God as the supreme ruler of the earth. God's kingship ("kingdom") was a dangerous denial of the omnipotence of the Roman emperor. For Mark, Jesus himself preached this reversal of power because he knew, in the ancient dual vision of the cosmos, that Satan, the real power behind the imperial throne and the priestly aristocracy beholden to it, was being vanquished by God's might. The victory starts with Jesus' success in his temptation in the desert (1:13) and continues throughout his ministry of healing and exorcism, his selfless death, to be completed at his glorious coming as the Son of Man.

From this point onward in the ministry of Jesus, there is no impediment to the healing and sanctifying presence of God to anyone who is willing to do God's kingly will because "this is the time of fulfillment." In contrast to the Baptist's more negative call (repentance for sin) and his preparatory role (he says "One mightier than I is coming after me"—1:7), Jesus' message is positive and definitive. It is the joyful announcement of freedom and life possible now that is summed up in Jesus' statement in 1:15: "This is the time of fulfillment. The kingdom of God is at hand. Repent, and believe in the gospel."

The first part of the proclamation, "This is the time of fulfillment," reads literally in the Greek: "The time [*kairos*] has been fulfilled" (1:15). *Kairos* is a word that has no English equivalent. As opposed to *chronos,* ordinary time, *kairos* means "an opportune moment, a welcome time of possibility." This idea of time occurs frequently in the Old Testament and means an eschatological time appointed by God, an opportunity for something to happen that fulfills part of God's great plan for salvation. For example, the prophet Ezekiel states, "The time has come," right after he says, "See, the day of the LORD! See, the end is coming" (Ezek 7:12 and 10; see also Isa 60:22; Dan 12:9; Zeph 1:12). The passive voice of the verb, "has been fulfilled," indicates that it was God who has brought about this special "*time of opportunity,*" an unrepeatable new segment of God's eternal plan which God has decided to inaugurate just now in the brand-new ministry of Jesus.

The content of Jesus' "gospel of God" is spelled out in Jesus' proclamation: "the Kingdom of God is at hand" (literally "has drawn near"). In this opportune time something new has happened, the Kingdom of God has already started to break in on the reality of Jesus' hearers. In the contemporaneous Essene community at Qumran a "Messiah of Righteousness" was expected to reign in "a covenant of kingship."[6] Here we can see the contemporaneous Jewish background of the "Kingdom" concept Jesus preaches, but he presents it as something radically new and unexpected.

The Kingdom of God is a force that breaks into the present from God's future and pushes us to "repent."[7] The "repentance" Jesus calls for is not the negative repentance for sin called for by John the Baptist, but rather a change of mind and heart, a complete change of mentality to a positive trust in the gospel ("Believe in the gospel"). "To believe" in Mark's Gospel means to entrust oneself to God's power in Jesus, as we see so often in the "belief" of those who trust that Jesus will cure them. Mark shows in the narrative that follows just what change is required for one to accept the Kingdom into one's life.

When Mark introduces Jesus' public ministry as starting in Galilee (1:14), he underlines the fact that Jesus started out on the *margins* of Jewish society, far away from where John the Baptist was preaching in the desert to "the whole Judean countryside and all the inhabitants of Jerusalem" (1:5). Jesus does not go first to the center of the official religion of the Temple, to the priests or any other recognized religious leaders. Instead, he goes far to the north of Jerusalem to his native Galilee, a place considered impure by the Temple aristocracy. Neither does he have anything to do with Rome's imperial cities of Sepphoris and Tiberias in Galilee, but he preaches in small towns like Nazareth and Capernaum, traditional Jewish enclaves where the common people lived. Thus, at the very beginning of Jesus' ministry, he shows that what God wants, "the Kingdom of God," is quite independent of the established religious and political power brokers. It is an alternative that God offers directly to the very ones marginalized by the aristocratic centers of power. Their violence against the poor is violence against God because it makes God's loving fatherhood hard to believe. It hinders God's benevolent will to create a life of freedom and justice in the world.[8]

SECTION A OF PART 1 OF THE GOSPEL (1:16–3:6)

The Gospel's first recorded act of Jesus after his preparation for ministry in the desert by the Holy Spirit is the rather implausible story of his call of four fishermen to follow him. Mark gives us no indication that Simon, his brother Andrew, and the Zebedee brothers, James and John, knew anything at all about Jesus. Yet, when he calls them with no more than a vague promise about making them (Peter and Andrew) "fishers of human beings," they leave their jobs and their families to follow him they know not where. Such a stark presentation of their call can only be a deliberate touch by the Evangelist to underline the profundity of the Christian vocation and the radicalness of its acceptance. For to follow Jesus, as the story will show, is to completely redefine your life.[9]

In the next narrative (1:21–28), the first of many miracles that Jesus would perform, Mark retells a traditional exorcism story in order to bring out the reality of the Kingdom in the activity of Jesus. Notice the repetition of the words "taught" (vv. 22, 27) and "authority" (vv. 22, 27) for emphasis. Jesus' teaching astonishes the hearers because of the "authority" with which

he accomplishes it, *his own* authority, and "not as the scribes," who habitu-
ally quote some earlier interpretation of the Law as their authority. But
before Mark gives us any actual instance of Jesus' teaching words, he recounts
Jesus' exorcism of an unclean spirit. The interpretive key here is the terrified
shout of the unclean spirit, "I know who you are—the Holy One of God!" (v.
24). Jesus is the "Holy One" because in his person the reign of Satan, the
power of Evil on earth, is being overcome. The holiness of Jesus is that God's
holy presence in Jesus, the Kingdom, clears the way for the return to society
of the possessed man whom the demon had made "unclean" or unholy. The
story doesn't give any specific defect or illness that made the man unclean
because Mark really wants to emphasize that the main problem of an
afflicted person is that he is unfit for participation in the religious and social
life of the community, "unclean," according to the Purity Code. Jesus is God's
"Holy One" because in him all uncleanness, or unholiness, is destroyed—
just as the demon feared.

The next little story shows the first of Jesus' many improprieties against the
Purity Code regarding women. According to the Mosaic Law, menstruation
made women "unclean," and it was highly improper for a "righteous" man ever
to touch any woman who was not part of his family, and so not familiar enough
with him to indicate her condition subtly. Jesus repeatedly breaks this "commandment" when he shows no partiality in his ministry, helping both men
and women equally in order to reinstate them into their proper roles in society. Here he touches Peter's fever-ridden mother-in-law so that she can perform the motherly task of preparing something to eat for the disciples (1:31).

Word of the healing spreads very fast in the small town of Capernaum so
that by evening people are bringing Jesus "all who were ill or possessed by
demons" (1:32). Such curative power as Jesus demonstrates is programmatic
of the arrival of the Kingdom, where God's loving presence proffers the
acceptance of all into a new and just society. So sensational is this "Good
News" that it could have derailed Jesus' ministry by its very effectiveness in
the lives of such ordinary, needy people. This danger does not escape Jesus
and he refuses to play to the masses and capitalize on his instant fame when
Peter points out: "Everyone is looking for you!" Jesus' response shows that he
is determined to stay on track with God's will. He will spread the Kingdom
by doing God's kingly will with no concern for himself. He responds, "Let us
go on to the nearby villages that I may preach there also. For this purpose
have I come" (1:38).

In the next story (1:40–45) Mark makes Jesus' agenda in presenting the
Kingdom very clear. In a long chapter in the Book of Leviticus God pre-
scribes to Moses and Aaron the social segregation necessary for anyone with
"leprosy," a generalizing name for any of a variety of ailments of the skin.[10]
Jesus touches a leper and cures him, telling him to "go, show yourself to the

priest and offer for your cleansing what Moses prescribed; that will be *proof* for them" (1:44). The miracle shows that God is inviting all people, even those afflicted by disease, to join the Kingdom. Since the man will obviously tell the priest that he had been made clean by Jesus' willing *touch,* Jesus will have proved that God's power (the Kingdom) has again bypassed the overly strict Purity Code. According to that code, the very act of the miracle (touching an unclean person) has made Jesus himself "unclean." Moreover, the miracle has taken place outside of the Temple and without its priests. *They* were able to do nothing to help the leper but could only excommunicate him when his malady befell him. They can reinstate him officially into society only if some *other* power (the power of God in Jesus) heals him.

Jesus, having himself become ritually unclean by his loving action, respects the prevailing custom and remains outside the towns "in deserted places." But when he keeps away from the synagogues where his "uncleanness" would cause a stir, the people respond by leaving their towns; they "kept coming out to him from everywhere" (1:45). In this way Mark begins to point out how subversive Jesus' preaching was to the established religious order.[11]

The Gospel's next five pericopes are a collection of Controversy Stories in which we see that the religious leadership not only does not understand Jesus' presentation of the Kingdom, but tries to thwart its arrival in his ministry. The first and last of these stories show the compassionate presence of God in Jesus whose power overcomes the spiritual and physical ailments of those who believe in him seeking healing. These two miracle stories, however, have a twist that reveals something more than Jesus' power to heal, for in them he calls himself "the Son of Man." In the first one (The Healing of a Paralytic, 2:1–12), Jesus proclaims that he, as the Son of Man, has the authority to forgive sins on earth. This means that in him God's own divine/heavenly power over sin is manifest. The scribes react, "Who but God alone can forgive sins?" They mean to say that sin can be forgiven only by what they consider to be God's system of reparation by sacrifice in the Temple, which they control. Jesus teaches them otherwise by curing the paralytic before their very eyes. The Kingdom of God that he preaches is clearly from God. It is God's powerful presence that has broken into the world to remedy the brokenness of humanity, something that the religious establishment was not even trying to do.

The second of the controversy stories (The Call of Levi, 2:14–17) begins a very important theme of Jesus' ministry, his table fellowship with the outcasts of society, with toll collectors, prostitutes, lepers, and others. Scholars point out that the sharing of a meal in the ancient world was extremely important in defining the boundaries of one's family or group. In particular, the Purity Code was very specific on issues of ritual purity when eating, automatically excluding any outsiders from table fellowship because of the uncleanness of their status, their profession, or their laxity about food regulations. Jesus again and again rejects this kind of exclusion and "recklessly violates any sense of decorum through his choice of table companions."[12] When the scribes challenge this, Jesus explicitly declares that he has "not come to call the righteous but sinners" into the Kingdom of God. Insofar as they proclaim themselves righteous, they are excluded from the Kingdom.

In the third Controversy Story (2:18–22) Jesus responds to the question of why his disciples did not fast. The practice of fasting, that is, of refusing to eat, was one way that people in ancient Judaism made a statement about their lives. While fasting is a religious action directed to God, it also speaks to and about the group to which one belongs. For example, fasting may be used to demonstrate to others how deeply one is mourning and begs for support from them in such distress. It may also be used as a valid religious excuse not to share table fellowship with those who are not of like mind and may thus strengthen the definition and unity of one's own group. When Jesus and the disciples do not fast, that is, when they eat anywhere and with anyone, they make a powerful statement to the scribes and the Pharisees that "they had no concern about upholding existing boundaries."[13]

The next story (Plucking Grain on the Sabbath, 2:23–28) shows Jesus using a story about the revered King David to point out the merciful intention of God's Law and the wrongness of the Pharisees' overly strict regulations for Sabbath observance. In an arresting statement Jesus reverses their view that religion subordinates believers to become the slaves of intolerant observance: "The sabbath was made for man, not man for the sabbath" (2:27). Then he adds that, as the heavenly Son of Man, he has God's authority over the Law, "the Son of Man is lord even of the sabbath" (2:28).

In the last controversy (The Man with a Withered Hand, 3:1–6), the shocked Pharisees do not give even a moment's consideration to the good that Jesus is doing in his healing ministry. Because of their impotence before the human frailty of the man's disability, all they can do is sit in ambush for the merciful Jesus to make a mistake he cannot explain. With both anger and sadness "at their hardness of heart," he must show them once again the proof of the presence of God in his ministry. "Stretch out your hand," (v. 5) he says to the paralytic, and the Pharisees receive the correct answer to sabbath observance. The useless hand is restored, and thus the man is restored to live his proper life, the one God wants him to have as God's beloved child.

In reality, all of these controversies show that Jesus' actions and his teachings burst the "old wineskins" (2:22) of the religious status quo of his opponents, the leaders of the prevalent legalistic and exclusionary religious practice. Mark demonstrates that Jesus does God's benevolent will while all the Pharisees can do is obsess about their overstrict religious prescriptions and despise the one who would circumscribe them. In Jesus the Kingdom arrives on the scene with the mercy of God to remedy the brokenness of humanity. On the one hand, the scribes and Pharisees cannot deny the reality of the miracles, and on the other they cannot convict Jesus of wrongdoing. So Mark points out that, as proof of their insincerity, their response to Jesus' new teaching was to plot together "with the Herodians against him to put him to death" (3:6).[14]

THE KINGDOM IN SECTION B OF PART 1 (3:7–6:6a)

In this next section of part 1 of the Gospel of Mark we notice an intensification of the struggle between Jesus and the religious authorities along with the rejection of his mission "in his native place and among his own kin and in his own house" (6:4). By contrast, the opening story (3:7–12) shows the appeal of Jesus to those outside the fold of Judaism (see v. 8). He readily accepts their presence even though many have come only because of his reputation as a healer. Now we see that the Kingdom Jesus preaches and makes present in his healing ministry is not restricted to members of the Jewish religion. Note how Jesus again rebukes the demons who would sidetrack his message by arousing the false hope that he was the kind of political Messiah/Son of God that people wanted (v. 11).

At this juncture in the narrative Jesus selects twelve special disciples "that they might be with him and he might send them forth to preach and to have authority to drive out demons" (3:14–15). Two points are important here: first, Jesus shows that the work of the Kingdom of God is a collaborative effort whereby God's saving power becomes present in God's Son, Jesus, and in those appointed by him to share his authority and witness. Here we learn that the nature of the Kingdom is such that it can only become effective in personal contact with believers, however imperfect their witness. This is why Mark presents Jesus' concern with food and sharing table fellowship so often, why he instructs his disciples on the meaning of parables (4:10–25), and why he teaches them the humility they will need to become great in service to the church (10:42–45).

The second point is the fact that the number of special coworkers that Jesus appoints is twelve. "Twelve" is a symbolic number that recalls the Twelve Tribes of Israel. Certainly Jesus is making a statement by choosing his special Twelve: what he is presenting is God's *official* offer to the Chosen People for the eschatological restoration of Israel.[15] The section concludes with another set of Controversy Stories (3:20–35) that we have already examined above in our chapter on Christology. In them we learn that Jesus' ministry is driven by the Holy Spirit and that his true family is in the Kingdom of God whose members are "whoever does the will of God" (3:35).

After the parable chapter, this section of the Gospel continues with several more miracles in which Mark further explains Jesus' identity. One important piece of information conveyed to the reader at the end is that Jesus cannot perform any miracle where there is no faith. Mark does not equivocate here; he makes it perfectly clear when he says, "he was *not able* to perform any mighty deed there. . . . He was amazed at their lack of faith" (6:5–6a). The power of God in Jesus, the dynamic healing quality of the Kingdom, is simply not active without the faith of the people involved.

SECTION C OF PART 1 OF THE GOSPEL (6:6b–8:26)

Here Jesus prepares his disciples for a radically new way of living. They must leave all security behind and, unencumbered by any "provisions," learn the key to God's will about how people are to interact: they are to share all they have. He sends them out to preach the Kingdom and to continue destroying the reign of Satan as they cast out his unclean spirits. It is essential for those who preach the gospel to believe in God and to trust in the generosity of those touched by God's Kingdom for the provision of the necessities of life. Therefore he commands the disciples to "take nothing for the journey but a walking stick—no food, no sack, no money . . . not a second tunic" (6:8–9) and to stay at whatever house will receive them. Only the acceptance of table fellowship and hospitality without restriction, no matter what accommodations one receives, can bring about the true sharing that the Kingdom requires. For, as Carlos Mesters has pointed out, "the Kingdom begins to exist when people, awakened by the message of Jesus, welcome others to share with them all they possess, so that they all become God's children, brothers and sisters of one another."[16]

In the two Miraculous Feeding Stories (6:34–44 and 8:1–9) the disciples urge Jesus to send the hungry crowds away to find something to eat, but Jesus tells them not to send people away in times of practical necessity. To truly follow Jesus means to share whatever you have. This is incomprehensible to the disciples who in both instances have only a few loaves of bread and a couple of fish. But when they share what they have, a miracle happens. There is plenty for everyone to eat, and an abundance of scraps left over. So it is in the Kingdom of God. When people share all they have in the task of spreading the Kingdom, they receive from the generosity and affection of people much more than they could ever have hoped for. As Jesus will later declare, "There is no one who has given up house or brothers or sisters or mother or father or children or lands for my sake and the sake of the gospel who will not receive a hundred times more now in this present age" (10:29–30).

After he has roundly condemned the Purity Code of the Pharisees and scribes in the discourse of 7:1–23, Jesus attempts to hide out in the non-Jewish district of Tyre (7:24), but he is not at all seeking to start a gentile mission. We remember that he refused the wish of the Gerasene demoniac, a Gentile, to "remain with him" and become a disciple (5:18). Nevertheless, a Syrophoenican woman in Tyre, who for Mark represents the entire "Greek" world, puts Jesus' principle of nonexclusivity to the test (7:24–30). When she begs for his help for her demonized daughter, Jesus answers metaphorically: his mission is for what every Jew would understand by "the children of God," his own Jewish people, not for the gentile "dogs." But when she replies cleverly with her own respectful yet demanding metaphor that "even the dogs under the table eat the children's scraps," (7:28) Jesus shows once and for all that God's Kingdom can have no restrictions—her daughter is healed.

Later on in part 3 of the Gospel Jesus is confronted with another kind of "outsider" in the person of a scribe in 12:28–34. Mark portrays these religious retainers of the priestly aristocracy as being the most antagonistic of Jesus' public opponents. Jesus boldly answers the scribe's question about the greatest commandment. The simple and striking answer is love of God and love of neighbor. The scribe recognizes the correctness of Jesus' response and confirms it with a Scripture citation of his own, affirming that love is much more important than the sacrificial system of the Temple cult that retains him. To this daring insight Jesus replies, "You are not far from the kingdom of God." The personal encounter with Jesus was disarming to anyone who was genuinely looking to find the Kingdom of God. At the same time, Jesus shows us that prejudice is completely disallowed in the Kingdom of God by acknowledging that even one of the group of his fiercest enemies can be on the right path to find God's will.

The Kingdom of God in the Parables of Jesus

In chapter 4 Mark presents a collection of lessons from Jesus' teaching, saying that Jesus always taught in such "parables" (4:33–34). By this term the Evangelist means a variety of image-filled sayings of the kind called *meshalim* (sing. *mashal*) in the Hebrew Old Testament. These metaphoric expressions include proverbs, one-liners, similitudes, and the slightly expanded versions of these types of sayings that occur in the Gospel.[17] Finally, Mark has chosen to relate two lengthy parables, namely, 4:3–8 and 12:1–11. There is a strong consensus among scholars that these *meshalim* all teach about the Kingdom of God, and so we shall make a brief comment on each one in this part of our study.

In the Gospel's first *mashal*, "Those who are well do not need a physician, but the sick do" (2:17), Jesus uses a proverb to explain his table fellowship with the sinners to whom he constantly proclaims the Kingdom of God. Mark loves to show the irony of Jesus' remarks. Does he think that the scribes do not need a physician, too?

In the question, "Can the wedding guests fast while the bridegroom is with them?" (2:19), Mark's Jesus here identifies himself as the bridegroom, implying that his presence is an occasion for rejoicing, because what he offers, the Kingdom of God, makes for a joyous time for all who would participate in it.[18] It is because of this new joyfulness that fasting is inappropriate, as is any holding back from the full communal celebration of all who believe in what Jesus has to say.

The two expanded proverbs about a new patch on an old piece of clothing and new wine in old wineskins (2:21–22) both dramatize the impossibility of grafting or inserting the total newness of the Kingdom into the old religious system. Fasting can be used to segregate some people from others, and that simply will not do. The proverbs expand the question, however, beyond the mere question of fasting, to the whole approach of what God wants in the Kingdom: the old system simply cannot bear the new freedom and inclusivity of Jesus' message.

The two proverbs about a divided kingdom and a divided house (3:24–27) set up Jesus' image of his task to tie up the strong man (Satan) and then plunder his house. In one of Mark's most vivid images, we see that in Jesus the power of God has broken into the world and incapacitated the rule of Satan. Although those who believe can still be tempted, Satan no longer has any *irresistible* power over them.

Mark has put together four separate *meshalim* in 4:21–25 in a double arrangement of two sayings each in the pattern: "[Saying 1] because [Saying 2]." The second saying of each pair gives an explanation of the first. The first *mashal,* "Is a lamp brought in to be placed under a bushel basket," (4:21) shows the clarifying nature of the Kingdom. When you bring it into your life it lights up everything in it, the good and the bad. Its power to change a person is total, and there is no area in which one can hold back, as the second member of the verse points out, "for there is nothing hidden except to be made visible; nothing is secret except to come to light" (4:22). The second double saying shows the reciprocal nature of embracing the Kingdom with regard to the benefits it brings to one's life: "The measure with which you measure will be measured out to you" (4:24). The blessings of the Kingdom far outreach our imagination, but refusal of it has dire consequences: "To the one who has, more will be given; from the one who has not, even what he has will be taken away" (4:25). These two statements of the consequences of holding back from the Kingdom will be felt immediately in one's life now. For it is the way one lives now that determines whether one is to "receive a hundred times more *now in this present age* [of] houses and brothers and sisters and mothers and children and lands" (10:30). That they are reserved for "Judgment Day" is unlikely, since Jesus never speaks of such a time in the Gospel of Mark.

The similitude of 4:26–29, The Seed Growing of Itself, is quite difficult to understand since the subject keeps shifting, from the farmer to the seed to the earth and back to the farmer again. Perhaps this is why both Matthew and Luke have chosen to omit it in their parable chapters. Clearly, however, this explicit comparison of the Kingdom to a farmer's seed shows that it is not the farmer who makes the seed grow. No, the Kingdom of God grows because of the presence of God in it, and should not be a cause of any false confidence on the part of its members. The addendum about the harvest in verse 29 changes the focus back to the farmer, but the farmer stands for God now. The harvest is not meant to be a threat to the Kingdom's members, but it is a hint as to the sureness and swiftness of God's final eschatological action.

The Similitude of the Mustard Seed (4:30–32) emphasizes the scope of God's plan. The Kingdom of God is worldwide in spite of its apparently humble beginnings in the carpenter from Nazareth. This metaphor of growth uses the mustard seed because of its tiny size, but some have noted Jesus' sense of humor here and elsewhere in the parables. The OT metaphor for the growth of God's People is an obvious allusion to the prophet Ezekiel's great cedar tree which "shall put forth branches and . . . / birds of every kind shall dwell . . . / in the shade of its boughs" (Ezek 17:23). In Jesus' parable, however, the Kingdom is like a mustard seed that only grows up to be a bush. It's a nice bush, a spicy bush, and a bush that can give shade to the proverbial birds of the air, just like the great cedar of Lebanon. But, after all, it is about as impressive to those who do not believe as the two-penny lamp in the *mashal* of 4:21. Perhaps we can see here a bit of humor at the grandiose pretensions of the religious establishment surrounding the Temple. Jesus teaches that, although it certainly appears to be something very simple, the apparent ordinariness of life in the Kingdom will enlighten the whole world and give refuge to every single person who needs its protection. As Carlos Mesters has pointed out, "The excluded and the marginalized must be welcomed, once again, into the intimacy of community, and thus know that they are welcomed by God."[19]

There may also be humor in the three conjoined one-liners in 9:49–50, where God's Kingdom is compared to the ridiculously simple and common substance of salt. The truth is that the ancient world without salt (it was the major preservative of food) would be a disaster, just as much as the race of human beings would be without the Kingdom of God.

We shall reserve our comments on the short parables of the Fig Tree (13:28) and the Returning Master (13:34–36) in the Eschatological Discourse in Mark's chapter 13 until our final chapter, which will examine that discourse thoroughly. Finally, we come to the two longer, allegorical, stories of the type that we normally think of when the subject of "parables" comes up. Interestingly, of the many rich parables of this type in the early traditions about Jesus, Mark chooses to report only two of them, considering both of them to be autobiographical of Jesus' ministry. In the parable of the Sower (4:3–8), Jesus highlights the results of his own task of "sowing" the Kingdom, and Mark adds the interpretation on Jesus' lips that the seed sown in the parable is "the word." The final parable, the Allegory of the Tenants (12:1–9), is explicitly autobiographical in its Marcan form. The Evangelist makes this clear when he humiliates "the chief priests, the scribes and the elders" (see 11:27) as they flee the scene in cowardice when they perceive that Jesus "had addressed the parable to them" (12:12).

The explanation of the parable of the Sower is in fact the key to all the parables, as Jesus points out by his saying in 4:13: "Do you not understand this parable? Then how will you understand any of the parables?" Mark highlights the importance of Jesus' clarification of the parables and frames it by the repetition of an imperative of Jesus in 4:9 and 23: "Whoever has ears to hear ought to hear!" This means, "If you really want to know what the Kingdom of God is about, then listen to what Jesus says in vv. 10–22!" Mark first tells us that "when he was alone, those present along with the Twelve questioned him about the parables" (v. 10). Throughout Mark's Gospel Jesus gives several "insider" explanations of his Gospel when he is "alone" with them (4:34; 7:33; 9:2, 28; 13:3), but here Mark includes "those present along with the Twelve." By this he is surely referring to his Christian community who are hearing this Gospel being read, for they are the ones who are truly present to Jesus in faith and just as interested in the parables as Jesus' first Twelve disciples.

Jesus says, "The mystery of the kingdom of God has been granted to you. But to those outside everything comes in parables" (v. 11). He preaches the Kingdom of God to *all*, but it is a mystery in that it requires more than a simple hearing to receive it. The enigma about the Kingdom, its mystery, is that one must *become a member of it* to understand it and any parable about it. Becoming a member of the Kingdom, of course, means having the faith to do God's will. This is the way of life that Jesus will explain in the rest of the Gospel: first the positive aspects of community sharing as a new family with special requirements, and then, by his own example, the hard fact that one must lose life to save it (8:35). Only such followers of Jesus who establish loving relationships in their living and suffering together can actively interpret his words.[20] "Those outside," in verse 4:11b, are those who put themselves outside God's grace by refusing to embrace God's will of justice and equality for all. They are condemned to hear the parables as unfathomable riddles, with the result that "they may look and see but not perceive," because they will not allow themselves to "be converted" to Jesus' new way of seeing reality and thus "be forgiven."

As Jesus continues his explanation of the parables, we remember that he does not discriminate in his invitation to the Kingdom. Therefore, the explanations of the different kinds of soil in the parable of the Sower refer not to the kinds of people (pure/impure, righteous/sinful, leaders/marginalized, and so on) who hear the word, but to their receptivity of the "seed" in the parable.[21] Jesus explains the allegory by saying, "The sower sows the word" (v. 14). The "word" here means the preaching of Jesus (as in 2:2 and 4:33), which is, of course, the good news about the Kingdom of God. Jesus points out that his preaching will not always be effective, even in those who willingly receive it, for there are three enemies of the kingdom: "Satan" himself, "tribulation or persecution," and "worldly anxiety, the lure of riches" (4:17, 19). These obstacles are programmatic of future episodes in the Gospel: in 8:33 Jesus declares that it is Satan who is leading Peter astray in his thinking from the human point of view; in 13:9–13 Jesus warns about coming persecutions and about tribulations in 13:7–8, 17, and 24; and in the story of the Rich Man in 10:17–22, it is his wealth that turns him away from following Jesus. Nevertheless, in the parable of the Sower, as indeed in the other two *meshalim* about seed that we have just seen, the ultimate triumph of God in the productive growth of the Kingdom is assured, "thirty and sixty and a hundredfold" (4: 20; cf. 8).

The two one-liners in verses 21–22 show the clarifying nature of the word of Jesus about the Kingdom of God. It lights the way for all those who take it to heart, but leaves in their darkness those who would hide it under a bushel. Eventually such denial of the will of God will take its toll, "for there is nothing hidden except to be made visible; nothing is secret except to come to light" (v. 22).

Turning to the second full-length parable, the parable of the Tenants (12:1–9), we note that a "vineyard" is a favorite metaphor for God's Chosen People in the Old Testament (e.g., Ps 80:9–17; Ezek 19:10–14). As a matter of fact, the descriptive imagery Jesus uses in the first verse of this parable is directly from the Vineyard Song of Isaiah 5:1–7. In the parable Jesus allegorizes that God, the owner of the vineyard, entrusted the vineyard of Israel to its religious leaders, but they produced no fruit for God. When God sent the prophets to them they abused and killed them. When finally God's own Son, Jesus, is sent to them, they plot to kill him. God's response is to put these tenants to death and give the vineyard to others. No wonder "the chief priests, the scribes and the elders" (introduced in 11:27) who "were seeking to arrest [Jesus]" turned away and left the scene. Jesus had just uncovered their plot to kill him, and "they realized that he had addressed the parable to them" (12:12). Mark undoubtedly has in mind that, after the resurrection, the Owner of the Vineyard will give that precious charge to Jesus' followers who will become "a house of prayer for all peoples" (11:17) and carry out God's will to preach the gospel to all nations (see 13:10).

The Kingdom of God in Part 2 of the Gospel

Only in the middle of the Gospel narrative does Jesus explain the necessity of his suffering and death (8:31–33). He realizes that his preaching of the Kingdom has been unmasking the error and corruption of the ruling religious leaders, and that he must go to their power center, Jerusalem, to complete his task. Since it is obvious to him that going up against such power will result in his death, he turns to his disciples to form them more fully so that they will be able to take up the cause of the Kingdom. First, he makes a journey through Galilee to consolidate the community of his followers (9:30–31), clarifying the criteria of how to enter and remain in the Kingdom. He then enters Judea (10:1) and makes more specific teachings on life in the Kingdom.[22] He teaches that there is to be no divorce, no amassing of power or great wealth, and no ambition except to serve one another.

In this second part and turning point of the Gospel, just after Peter correctly identifies him as the Messiah, Jesus makes the unambiguous statement that his Messiahship is one of suffering. It is God's will that it be so: "the Son of Man *must* suffer greatly . . . and be killed" (8:31). For Jesus, only God's will *must* be done. In a blunt response to Peter's objection, he says that to deny this truth is the work of Satan and purely human thinking (8:31–33). Moreover, Jesus says that those who wish to come after him, that is, those who want to be his true disciples, "must deny [themselves], take up [their] cross, and follow me," even to the death (8:34–35). This new dimension of Jesus' teaching takes Peter by surprise, but for the readers of the Gospel it has been foreshadowed early on in the story. We recall the murderous reaction against Jesus of the Pharisees together with the Herodians in 3:6 and the execution of John the Baptist (6:14–29), the one who prepared Jesus' way, and whose body was also "laid . . . in a tomb" (6:29; cf. 15:46).

The stakes are high for one who has heard the call to God's Kingdom, for in denying it one would "forfeit his life" even if one would "gain the whole world" (8:36). Of that person "the Son of Man will be ashamed . . . when he comes in his Father's glory with the holy angels" (8:38). Even if Jesus does not know when *that* is to happen (see 13:32), he does know that "there are some standing here who will not taste death until they see that the kingdom of God has come in power" (9:1). From the point of view of the Gospel this can only mean that some event(s) in the near future will manifest the Kingdom in a way heretofore unseen, that is, that the Kingdom will arrive "in power."

There has been an enormous amount of speculation on when this coming of the Kingdom *in power* was supposed by Mark (and by Jesus) to take place. Mark's mention of the Coming of the Son of Man in the preceding verse (8:38) has given rise to a plethora of opinions on the timing of this part of God's plan. It is the task of this book to sort out just how the

Evangelist used his traditions about the words and deeds of Jesus to explain God's entire eschatological program. This secret plan includes Jesus' necessary suffering and death, his resurrection, the coming of the Kingdom of God in power, the persecutions and suffering of Jesus' followers in the postresurrection period, their death and resurrection, and the final return of Jesus in glory. Mark makes clear that during his ministry Jesus was able to predict each part of God's plan, although the *timing* of the very last act, the Coming of the Son of Man from heaven, is known to God alone (13:32).

I have already examined the first two parts of this timeline, namely, the public ministry of Jesus and his prediction of his suffering and death. The final part of this book will deal with the future, that is, the eschatology of the followers of Jesus, as well as his final Coming from heaven. I shall identify the timeline of "the Kingdom of God come in power," next, after an examination of a few more texts that concern the nature of the Kingdom.

In 9:43–48 Mark has put together three sayings on the avoidance of sin in which Jesus seems to advocate self-mutilation rather than surrender to the temptation to sin. It would be clear to any first-century Christian reader that Jesus is not to be taken literally here. Such mutilation is strictly forbidden by the Law of God in the Old Testament. The language, of course, is figurative; it is what we would call "hyperbole," an exaggerated mode of speech. It is used here to place the highest emphasis on the avoidance of sin in the three areas of human activity, what anthropologists call the three human "zones of interaction" with the world, represented by the hand, the foot, and the eye.[23]

What is of interest for our study in these three sentences is the parallel use of the phrase "to enter into life" (vv. 43, 45) with the phrase "to enter into the kingdom of God" (v. 47). In contrast to "life/Kingdom," the result of sin in each of the three sayings is "to go/be thrown into Gehenna" (43, 45, 47). Gehenna (for Hebrew *ge-hinnom* "the valley of Hinnom") is the name of the valley west of Jerusalem used as a garbage dump, whose perpetual fires came to symbolize the eternal punishment of sinners in Jewish literature.

The word used for "life" (*zōē*) is used elsewhere in Mark only twice, both times in the phrase "eternal life." "Eternal life" is characterized as an inheritance (something future) resulting from proper living in 10:17, and a property of "the age to come" in 10:30. For this reason many think that "life" in verses 43 and 45 refers to eternal life, and thus that its parallel "the Kingdom" (in v. 47) means some reward after death. But this is to misunderstand the Kingdom. "Life" in the Bible means the true human life, one lived in close relationship with God and in which one enjoys God's goodness.[24] This being fully alive and living life as God meant it in the present is put into strong contrast with "eternal life" in the saying: "There is no one who has given up house or brother . . . who will not receive a hundred times more now *in this present age . . . and* eternal life *in the age to come*" (10:29–30). Although the saying in 9:47 about the Kingdom has a future cast to it, we conclude that it means "life" in the immediate future of the believer. This is confirmed by three more instances of the phrase "enter into the Kingdom" in Mark 10. Here, at the end of part 2 of the Gospel, two sets of sayings on the Kingdom are very instructive in that they run strictly counter to the prevailing social norms about children and about the rich. In the ancient world, while children were revered and loved because they guaranteed the family line and provided security in their parents' old age, when they were young they had no rights and little status. In fact, they were no more than slaves in a family, and they couldn't inherit the estate as long as they were still minors.[25]

When some parents brought their children to Jesus so that he could touch them (probably to ward off evil from harming them), the disciples tried to chase them away as not being worthy of the Teacher's time (10:13). But Jesus became angry and did even more than the parents had asked for the children. He blessed them and embraced them, "for the kingdom of God belongs to such as these" (10:14). Not content with that single affirmation, the Evangelist reinforces it with the solemn statement of Jesus in the next verse, "Amen, I say to you, whoever does not accept the kingdom of God like a child will not enter it." What this scene describes is far from some modern romantic notion of a child's innocence or imaginative playfulness. Jesus means that the Kingdom will be made up of people who live like the children of his time, those who have no power of their own, no "rights," no possible claim to such an inheritance.

The story of the Rich Man (10:17–22) can only be properly understood in light of the economy of first-century Palestine. In a zero-sum economy one can only become rich at someone else's expense. Great personal wealth was always the result of some unjust actions by the powerful elites, or their brokers, who controlled the economy, the judicial system, and the police. Even if one inherited one's riches they were still considered ill-gotten by the poor who were constantly being exploited by the system.[26]

When the man asks about "eternal life," Jesus' response focuses on just this point when he substitutes the commandment "You shall not defraud" for the expected "You shall not covet" in the Ten Commandments. The man demonstrates his blindness to the truth when he protests that he has observed all the commandments from his youth. In spite of this Jesus recognizes his vulnerability in asking the question and recognizes a possible moment of conversion.[27] Rather than condemn his hypocrisy Jesus "looking at him, loved him." Responding to his genuine need, he gives him the honest answer to his question about eternal life: "Go, sell what you have, and give it to [the] poor" (10:21). "Eternal life," or "treasure in heaven" as Jesus calls it in verse 21, comes only to those who enter the Kingdom now, when they give up the privilege and power that wealth guarantees. When he asks what he needed to *do* to "inherit eternal life," the man doesn't realize that one has to give up the *power to do*, especially the power of wealthy, and become like a child to rely totally on God to enter the Kingdom. The man goes away, and thus declines to follow Jesus as a disciple, "sad, for he had many possessions" (10:22). This is tragic for Jesus, too; he turns to his disciples and laments, "How hard it is for those who have wealth to enter the kingdom of God" (10:23).

The disciples are surprised by this comment about the Kingdom, and so he tries to teach them by repeating himself. He uncharacteristically calls them "children" to remind them of what he has just said about the effortless entrance into the Kingdom of powerless children. So he lays it out clearly for them: "It is easier for a camel to pass through [the] eye of [a] needle than for one who is rich to enter the kingdom of God" (10:25). True enough, for nowhere else in the Gospel does Jesus ask someone to follow him who had come to him on their own, and nowhere else do we see anyone departing from Jesus after having been called to follow, "for he had many possessions" (10:22).

The disciples are "exceedingly astonished" at Jesus' words because in the ancient Circum-Mediterranean society where patronage determined wealth, the rich were considered to be blessed by the chief patron, God, whose will it must have been that they were so prosperous. Moreover, only the rich could afford to pay all their tithes, their Temple taxes, and pay for all the sacrifices that the Purity Code required. What Jesus says about the Kingdom here completely overturns the common wisdom of this society and causes the flummoxed disciples to groan, "Then who can be saved?"

The disciples still do not understand the radical difference of Jesus' teaching about giving up control and sharing all that one has. Going on their previous assumptions, they simply infer that if the rich can hardly be saved, the rest of society has no chance at all. Only when one understands that there can be no power in the Kingdom besides God's, can one be a member of it. As for earthly prosperity, it can only come about for all when all are willing to share what they have, however little they think it might be. Jesus then assures his disciples that there will never be anyone who has given up family and possessions "for my sake and the sake of the gospel," who cannot justly expect to "receive a hundred times more now in this present age." In the community formed by the Kingdom of God, family and land and all else are shared, not plundered. As to "eternal life," that is guaranteed also "in the age to come" (v. 30).

We can hardly believe it when, after Jesus goes on to announce his passion and death for a second time (10:33–34), the disciples James and John naively reveal their ambition and ask for lordship in the Kingdom. We don't know exactly what kind of scenario these sons of Zebedee are thinking of when they ask Jesus to "grant that in your glory we may sit one at your right and the other at your left" (10:37), but Jesus does not deny that he is destined for glory with attendants at each side. However, it is God who will judge and reward as God wills, since it is God who has prepared the glorious reward to be shared with Jesus (10:40). Jesus makes very clear again that they, like all of his followers, must first share in his suffering service to the community of believers in order to be great (10:44; cf. 8:34–38).

The Passion Narrative

At the beginning of the final part of the Gospel, Jesus formally enters Jerusalem riding on a donkey colt that he had specifically requested, in symbolic fulfillment of Zech 9:9, where the humble king and savior is expected to come in peace "meek, and riding on an ass, / on a colt, the foal of an ass." The crowd receives him joyfully as "he / who comes in the name of the LORD," quoting the blessing of the priests upon the victorious king in Ps 118:26. They shout their blessing upon "the kingdom of our father David that is to come" (11:10), but that is the wrong kingdom! The very next sequence of events proves this. Jesus curses a fig tree, but before we see that it becomes "withered to its roots," (11:20) Mark portrays Jesus purging the Temple of its moneychangers. Mark frequently "sandwiches" one story into another, using a literary device called *intercalation* to relate two originally separate stories, showing that the one incident sheds light on the meaning of the other. Here the withered fig tree symbolizes the Temple, the power base of the leaders of the religious establishment who seek a political kingdom as glorious as that of King David once was. Jesus attacks this Temple, calling it a robbers' den, an evil lair devoid of all prayerful worship of God, sterile as a completely desiccated fruit tree. Its economic tyranny against the poor has been called "an act of violence against God" because it attacks the credibility of God's Fatherhood and affirmation of life.[28]

In a narrative tour de force from 11:27 to 12:34, Mark goes on to show how Jesus confounds each group of the religious leadership that oppresses the people with their Temple sacrifice system and Purity Code. In one argument after the other, Jesus takes on the chief priests, the scribes, and the elders, along with the Pharisees and Sadducees, and completely baffles them by his understanding of God's Kingdom. In 12:35–37 Jesus shows that the true Messiah is certainly not to be the scion of David, as the religious leaders presumed. No, the popular idea of the "Kingdom of David," its Temple, and its religious leaders—from the aristocracy of the chief priests to the tradition-bound Pharisees—definitely do not belong to the Kingdom of God.

The next segment of the Gospel is the great Eschatological Discourse of chapter 13. Having denounced the scribes for their insidious exploitation of the resources of widows (12:38–44), Jesus unequivocally condemns their power source, the Jerusalem Temple, to total destruction (13:2). He goes on to solemnly warn his followers of the afflictions and persecutions that will befall them as they preach the gospel to all nations before the End (13:10). They are his servants who must be ever at their work, not knowing when the Lord will return (13:34–35). Although it is of great concern to us, the question of the exact relation of the Kingdom of God and the Second Coming of Jesus is not discussed in the Eschatological Discourse. We shall examine that Discourse thoroughly in the last part of this book, when we will make our final conclusions on the timetable of God's plan announced by Jesus.

When we come to the scene of the Last Supper (14:22–25), Mark describes Jesus' most powerful prophetic and symbolic action concerning the Kingdom of God. In the context of a Passover meal, Jesus gives the ultimate example of the total sharing required by God's Kingdom. Here Jesus declares that his body and blood, that is, the total gift of his life, will ratify the new covenant. At this ritual meal that began as a remembrance of the old covenant, he gives the eucharistic bread, his body, as the nourishment of his new covenant people, and the wine, his blood, as the seal of their new covenant.[29]

At the conclusion of the meal Jesus makes a solemn declaration that he will no longer be able to feast with his disciples "until the day when I drink it [wine] new in the kingdom of God" (14:25). Here he assures them that, although he must die, neither his presence to the community nor the Kingdom itself will be terminated by his death.[30] He has already predicted three times (8:31; 9:31; 10:34) that after his death he will be raised up again to life. Now he clarifies that he will return to them in the Kingdom to drink the new wine that bursts the old wineskins (see 2:21), that is to say, that it is precisely by his death and resurrection that the Kingdom will come about in a more definitive way.[31]

The final mention of the phrase "kingdom of God" in the Gospel comes after Jesus' death. In 15:43 Mark introduces the person who asked Pilate for the corpse of Jesus for burial as Joseph of Arimathea, "who was himself awaiting the kingdom of God." This enigmatic description in Mark has given rise to the full range of interpretations. He is seen in a favorable light in the later Gospels. For Matthew, Joseph was "himself a disciple of Jesus" (Matt 27:57); he was "secretly a disciple of Jesus" in John 19:38. Finally, in Luke he "had not consented to [the Sanhedrin's] plan of action [to crucify Jesus]" (Luke 23:51). Many recent scholars, however, speculate that the historical Joseph may have been concerned merely that the Purity Code not be violated by having a Jewish corpse left unburied after sundown.[32]

Our question, of course, is what *Mark* thought about this tradition, and especially what he meant by Joseph's relation to the Kingdom. It seems very likely, given Mark's love of irony, that the Evangelist added a twist to the tradition about the person who did for Jesus what the disciples failed to do, namely, to bury his corpse. When we read this episode as written before the other Gospel accounts in which Joseph is shown in a favorable light, and thus independent of them, we see several factors that indicate Mark's negative opinion of Joseph's actions. First, Joseph, "a distinguished member of the council," was part of the Sanhedrin trial in which Mark says "they *all* condemned him as deserving to die" (14:64). Second, he "*courageously* went to Pilate and asked for the body of Jesus" (15:43), because by doing it he risked being associated with the one who was executed as an illegitimate royal pretender, a traitor to Rome, "the king of the Jews." Third, after confirming that Jesus was dead, Pilate handed over the corpse to Joseph, because he knew him as one of the Sanhedrin, the most powerful religious institution that collaborated with Roman rule. Finally, in Mark's account Joseph does none of the proper burial rites of washing and anointing, but disposes of the corpse by wrapping it in a simple cloth of linen and placing it into a makeshift rock grave. He needs to roll a stone over it to prevent any future ritual impurity by wild animals desecrating the corpse. Thus Joseph, one of the religious elite, is merely carrying out the Law's prescription to bury the corpse of a criminal who has been publicly executed: "You shall bury it the same day; otherwise, since God's curse rests on him who hangs on a tree, you will defile the land" (Deut 21:23). The Marcan irony is that this righteous deed was done by a person who was seeking the Kingdom wrongly, since he would have nothing to do with the Kingdom Jesus preached, but condemned him to death. Joseph may have been awaiting the Kingdom of God, but he was still one of "those outside" it (see 4:11).

Mark underscores the difficulty that Jesus' followers have in understanding his way of suffering when all the disciples abandon him at his arrest in Gethsemane (14:50). They will be forgiven for their cowardly act when, after the timeline of Mark's story, they regather to preach the Kingdom and found the Jesus movement, the church of which this Gospel is a part. Mark understands this forgiveness well, for the "young man" who was "wearing nothing but a linen cloth about his body" (14:51) at Jesus' arrest in Gethsemane may well be an autobiographical allusion to the Evangelist himself, as many scholars have speculated. Mark may be recalling a shameful and cowardly time in his life, using the image of himself literally jumping out of his clothes to run away from the suffering of Jesus. But at the end of the Gospel, this same "young man" returns, and once more "clothed in a [his baptismal?] white robe," at the scene of the Empty Tomb. There he has the privilege of proclaiming the resurrection to the women and instructing them to further announce the Good News (16:6–7)—exactly as Mark has done for us by writing this Gospel!

After the young man announces the resurrection of Jesus to the women at the empty tomb, he charges them to tell the disciples, "He is going before you to [in] Galilee; there you will see him, as he told you" (16:7). Indeed, just after the Last Supper Jesus had admonished them that they all "will have your faith shaken" by his death, but that "after I have been raised up, I shall go before you to [in] Galilee" (14:27–28). We translate the prepositional phrase "to [in] Galilee" thus ambiguously because, as so often the case, our Evangelist here uses language that can have two or more meanings. The young man's statement in 16:7 can mean that Jesus is preceding them *to* Galilee, meaning that it is there that they also should go to encounter their resurrected Lord.[33]

In a better interpretation, however, the young man's announcement can mean that Jesus will go before them *in* Galilee, that is, he will be *leading* them there as a shepherd leads his flock (cf. 14:27). This will happen, however, only if they go back to "Galilee," a place that has a powerful symbolic meaning in this Gospel, both here at its end and at its beginning ("Galilee" is mentioned five times in chap. 1). "Galilee," the locale where Jesus started his ministry, has both a geographic and a theological meaning in Mark. It is far from the center of the official Jewish religion, actually on its margins, and is considered an impure place by the religious leaders. Here we should understand that the disciples may "see" Jesus only if they dare to go back to the symbolic Galilee, that is, if they return to the "beginning" of the Gospel. Like Jesus, they must reach out to the poor and outcast on the margins of society, share all they have with them, and then pass through their own "Passion Narrative" as they suffer with Jesus in spreading the Kingdom. This is the demand Mark sets out for every true Christian disciple: to have the same attitude toward conflict as Jesus, that is, to embrace it in love as did the One who was completely free in his fidelity to God's will.[34] It is a life experience that no resurrection appearance story can cause or be a substitute for. This is why the Gospel ends abruptly at 16:8 (original ending), with no appearance of the resurrected Jesus needed to conclude it.[35]

THE TIMING OF THE KINGDOM

Now we turn to the very knotty problem of the timeline of the Kingdom of God, to a summary of what our Evangelist presupposes and clarifies for us about what we have learned so far about when and how the Kingdom comes. We must first admit that we cannot expect an airtight consistency in this matter, nor should we insist on a single-faceted logic when we know that this ancient writer has edited many sources in presenting his own personal understanding of the Kingdom. Our procedure will be to line up the data in the Gospel about the arrival of the Kingdom, and then make a summary of what we have found.

The first use of the phrase "the Kingdom of God" in the Gospel sets the theme for the whole of its first part (1:16–8:26). A literal translation of the text is: "The time has been fulfilled and the Kingdom of God has drawn near" (1:15). Here Mark's Jesus uses two verbs in the perfect tense in Greek, the tense that signifies that although something has happened already in the past, its effect perdures and influences the present. Thus, as we have stated above, "the time has been fulfilled" (Mark 1:15) means that the date for some special event in God's plan has come to pass; the event has already begun.

The verb in the second clause, "has drawn near" *(engiken),* is greatly controverted, but this is because many scholars cannot shed their quantitative, future-oriented perception of time. The Greek verb itself derives from the adverb "near" and means, in the perfect tense, "has drawn near" in the sense of "has already come near and is now at hand." The implication of what Jesus is saying is that the Kingdom of God is close to all and can become present *now* in the experience of all who follow him. The Gospel shows again and again in the ministry of Jesus how the Kingdom of God *does* break into the lives of those who believe in him. Such confidence in God's presence in Jesus makes them whole, driving out the evil that haunts them, and returns them to their proper place in the society from which they had been marginalized.

In chapter 4 of the Gospel, as we have seen, the nature of the Kingdom is explained in the parables. In 4:11 Jesus speaks of the mysteriousness of the Kingdom, and in 4:26 and 30 the God-directed growth of the Kingdom is assured by the similitudes of the Seed Growing by Itself and the Mustard Seed. So also in the Kingdom sayings in 9:47; 10:14–15, 23–25, the Kingdom is spoken about as something that one can enter, a reality present to the experience of those wish to participate in it. The scribe in 12:34 and Joseph of Arimathea (15:43) are still outside the Kingdom because of their incomplete faith. All these verses in which the Kingdom is spoken about refer to its demands for the present time. They are the demands of a reality that is already in existence, accessible immediately to those who believe and dedicate themselves to God's will. Some will never enter the Kingdom of God; they are "those outside" (4:11). Others who at first enter it will leave it for a variety of reasons (4:14–19).

In only two verses about the Kingdom of God, 9:1 and 14:25, is something exclusively in the future spoken about, but—and this is very important—in neither case is the Kingdom itself said to be exclusively future. In 14:25, as we have seen, Jesus promises to return to the fellowship of the disciples and drink new wine after his resurrection, but he does not clarify just when that moment "in the Kingdom of God" will be. In 9:1, on the other hand, Jesus predicts that some standing with him will "see that the kingdom of God has come in power." This evidently means that these people will see something new, something different from the effect of the Kingdom on those who have already experienced it in the ministry of Jesus, in his already powerful words and deeds. The something new is that the Kingdom will come *in power,* and the key to understanding when that will happen is the context of 9:1, beginning with Jesus' statement on the Coming of the Son of Man in glory (8:38), and including the following account of the Transfiguration (9:2–8).

First of all, it is very unlikely that 9:1 would simply repeat the statement of the previous verse (8:38) in different words, and so the coming of the Kingdom "in power" (9:1) *is being contrasted* here with the Coming of Jesus in glory as the Son of Man (8:38). Mark is saying that the Kingdom must come in power *before* the Second Coming, that *final* event in history, when the Son of Man "will send out the angels and gather [the] elect" from the ends of the world (13:27). That event can only happen after the destruction of the Temple (13:2) and after much tribulation (13:24), when the elect will have preached the gospel to all nations (13:10). But when does the Kingdom *first* come "in power"?

The fact that 9:1 is followed by the account of the Transfiguration is very significant. It appears that Mark is explaining the rather enigmatic statement in 9:1 by the following verses (9:2–13). Here Jesus goes up a mountain with his inner circle of disciples, Peter, James, and John, and briefly appears to them in all his heavenly glory. In this vision, time and space are collapsed when Jesus speaks with the heavenly figures from the ancient past, Moses and Elijah, his great prophetic predecessors. It is a glimpse of the celestial reality of the glory of Jesus that stands behind his *apparently* fragile earthly reality in the final days of his ministry.

At the end of this Transfiguration scene we find the key to the timing of the coming of the Kingdom of God "in power." Jesus admonishes the disciples "not to relate what they had seen to anyone, except when the Son of Man had risen from the dead" (9:9). Only after the resurrection could people possibly understand the meaning of Jesus' heavenly reality, a fact that proved to be true even for those disciples who themselves witnessed the Transfiguration. They obviously did not understand it, or they would never have run away when Jesus was arrested in Gethsemane.

What does it mean, then, to say that the Kingdom was to come *in power?* In the Gospel of Mark the word "power" (*dynamis* in Greek) always refers to the power over life and death of a living, active God. In 6:2, 5, 14; 9:39 the word means a "mighty deed" of God's power, what we would call a "miracle." In 12:24 it refers to the power of God to raise the dead; in 13:26 Jesus will come as the Son of Man with divine power and glory. In 14:62 the phrase "seated at the right hand of the Power" uses *dynamis* as a reverential substitute for God's name at the coming of the Son of Man and clearly means that Jesus will be seated at the right hand of *God.*

We conclude that for Mark the Kingdom of God has already drawn near at hand in the time of fulfillment that Jesus announced at the beginning of his public life. It was present in Jesus *throughout* his healing and teaching ministry. It became present *in power* after the two-sided event of Jesus' self-giving death and God's eschatological vindication of him in the resurrection.[36]

In Mark's theology the disciples could only begin to understand the real identity of Jesus after his death and resurrection. Indeed, when Jesus dies, even a pagan centurion at the foot of the cross proclaims that Jesus is "Son of God" (15:39). But only after God's powerful act of overcoming death itself in raising Jesus to new life could anyone understand the true nature of the Cross. This double cosmic event of Jesus' cross and resurrection brings about a new phase in God's plan, one in which believers can understand the true power of God. Thus empowered by this final disclosure of the identity of Jesus (the full revelation of the Messianic Secret!) his followers could begin to comprehend God's plan for the salvation of all humanity by their own obedient discipleship. Their entrance into the Kingdom of God on earth is their compliance with God's will that "the gospel must first be preached to all nations" (13:10).[37] Then they will become God's new "house of prayer for all peoples" (11:17), after they encounter Jesus "in Galilee" where they will make his spiritual journey their own, themselves empowered by the leadership of the risen Jesus. In this new phase of the Kingdom, the church's eucharistic celebrations will be a joyous fellowship with Jesus, just as surely as the banquet of the Last Supper was a prophecy and symbol of his death.[38] This, truly, was when the Kingdom first came "in power"!

SUMMARY AND CONCLUSIONS

In the Gospel of Mark, the Kingdom of God is a totally new existential reality for the covenant people of Israel, which God has brought near in the ministry of Jesus. It is not a place, and certainly not "heaven,"[39] but a mysterious and hidden state of being at this point in time, because it is an interaction with God, attainable in a person's life only by faith. In it men and women together may enjoy the grace of God's holy presence to them as supreme ruler of their lives and restorer of their freedom and salvation. Although Jesus announced the Kingdom to Israel, it was impossible to deny it to others who sought the lordship of Israel's loving God, for it is the destiny of all, "the possibility of a new and just society, worthy of human beings, the alternative that God proposes to humanity."[40]

The Kingdom's beginnings were in Galilee, far from the rule of Temple and Law, and indeed, quite subversive of the exclusionism of the established religious leaders. They tried to thwart its beginning, for it was clear that the

Kingdom could not fit their legalistic and elitist socioreligious system. In his ministry Jesus continually contrasted the Kingdom's power to save over against the impotence of their legalism. He made it clear that it would not be entrusted to them, would not be hindered by their Purity Code, but that it was a *new* covenant relation between God and the Chosen People. The religious leaders' inevitable reaction to Jesus as revealer of the Kingdom was one of violence: the one whom they could not defeat in argument they had to kill!

As God's Son, Jesus had the authority to announce the Kingdom, and it began to break into earthly existence from the heavenly realm of God's absolute power with Jesus as its center. This is the power that heals infirmity and casts out the evil that cripples humanity, binding people with the power of sin, cutting them off from their rightful inheritance as children of God. It pushes in from the future to break down all the religious and social barriers that divide society and oppress those marginalized by the prevailing politicoreligious system.[41]

Although it is not a geographical locale, the Kingdom is a dimension of being in which those who believe can dwell. It is a community that replaces the patriarchal family in its support and concern for its members. What is required for entrance into this new state of being is repentance, a radical change from a life of despair and the fatalistic acceptance of injustice to one of trust in God's loving and liberating presence. Entrance into the Kingdom of God means entering God's eschatological plan where a life of total sharing with others means a life in the proper relationship with God. As loving Father, God forgives all but also demands total forgiveness of one another. The mystery of the Kingdom is this: one must enter it, that is, commit oneself to God's will by faith, in order to understand what God really wants for each person. Otherwise, life remains an unsolvable riddle for the poor and powerless, and an empty hypocrisy for the rich and powerful.

This reality that Jesus proffers appears to be something very simple, like salt, or a mustard seed, and it takes place in ordinary life. In the Kingdom God's loving presence destroys all impediments, be they physical, social, emotional, or spiritual, to union with one's true community. Driven by the Holy Spirit, it is a new and totally inclusive family, with prejudice toward none. All its members must collaborate to announce it and bring it about by their preaching of the gospel to all nations. In fact, it depends on God's love that works through the generosity of those who are truly seeking God's will.

To remain outside it, by embracing any other reality but God as one's security, is to continue to live in the fear and shame of a life dominated by sin. To deny the Kingdom, or to leave it—one is always free (and even tempted) to do so—is in fact to forfeit one's life, since the Messianic banquet is prepared only for those who follow Jesus by preaching his gospel of justice and belonging for all.

The Evangelist Mark is like a good friend in a time of suffering. He does not speak much of the joy of entering the Kingdom now as do the other Evangelists. In fact, in his Gospel Jesus says that it will be a time of fasting when he, the bridegroom, is gone (2:20). Neither does Mark recount Jesus' stories of God's tender love, like the parables of the Prodigal Son and the Lost Sheep, or the nearness of the Branches to the Vine. No, to us and to his deeply afflicted community he tells it like it is: times are terribly difficult now. There doesn't seem to be any relief in sight. Like Jesus, their preaching of gospel justice will cause them to be baptized with the baptism of suffering in lives of selfless service of others that will take them to their own "Galilee" experience of rejection and persecution. Rejection and persecution are, in fact, the fate of all who follow Jesus. Didn't Jesus say that his true followers must "take up [their] cross" and lose their life "for my sake and that of the gospel" (8:34–35)? The true disciple must follow Jesus' ministry of suffering service and the total gift of himself that he so perfectly prefigured at the Last Supper and carried out in the crucifixion.

So what is the payoff for exchanging a despicable but predictable life of marginalization and impotent exploitation by the powers of this world for one of rejection, affliction, and uncertainty for the sake of the gospel of Jesus? The difference couldn't be greater! Disciples of Jesus, as members of the Kingdom, will be consoled and protected by God's love in a community of brothers and sisters, a hundredfold of the realities that make life meaningful in this age. True, they will suffer, perhaps even more in the present life than if they had ignored Jesus' urgent message. But if they make the leap into the Kingdom with Jesus, they will live for what God created them for, free and confident. No matter the cost, the gift of their lives of other-centered service will culminate in their salvation and eternal life in the age to come.

Although its profound reality could be perceived only after the resurrection, when the Kingdom of God came in power, the death of Jesus is humanity's moment of glory, for in it God's infinite power of loving mercy is most clearly seen. In fact, the sacrifice of Jesus on the cross is the most revealing moment in God's plan, for it is the total self-offering of God to humanity. For while God always has complete power over life and death, the crucifixion of Jesus is the pledge that we humans are totally free to accept God's love as offered by the obedient Son of God—or to reject it out of hand as we wish. The resurrection of Jesus is first of all God's validation of the way Jesus lived and died.

The Kingdom of God has come in power in Jesus' death and resurrection, just as he predicted, and the holiness of God has come near to all who suffer in Jesus' name. It is God's power that guarantees the Kingdom's growth, and God's unknown schedule that will bring it to fulfillment. Jesus, the true representative of humanity, is its model who lives the fullness of human being in freedom and total confidence in God. But Jesus has promised that he will come, as the Son of Man, "in his Father's glory with the holy angels" and gather his elect (8:38). It is to this, the eschatological theme of the Gospel, that we must now turn in the second part of our study.

NOTES

1. Aloysius M. Ambroczic, *The Hidden Kingdom: A Redactional-Critical Study of the References to the Kingdom of God in Mark's Gospel* (CBQMS 2; Washington, D.C.: Catholic Biblical Association, 1972), 244.

2. The phrase "the Kingdom of God" occurs fourteen times in the Gospel of Mark (1:15; 4:11, 26, 30; 9:1, 47; 10:14, 15, 23, 24, 25; 12:34; 14:25; 15:43).

3. The texts are 1 Chr 28:5; 2 Chr 13:8; Wis 10:10 and Pss 103:19; 145:11, 12, 13; 1 Chr 17:14; cf. 29:11; Dan 4:3, 34; 7:27; cf. 2:44.

4. Joseph A. Fitzmyer, *The Gospel according to Luke* (Anchor Bible 28; New York: Doubleday, 1981), 155.

5. See Fitzmyer's comments on "God's Gospel" in his Anchor Bible Commentary, *Romans* (New York: Doubleday, 1993), 109–10.

6. This statement is found in a document of the Dead Sea Scrolls called "the Patriarchal Blessings" (1QPB 2).

7. So Guillermo Cook and Ricardo Foulkes, *Marcos: Comentario Biblico Hispanoamericano* (Miami: Editorial Caribe, 1993), 68.

8. Carlos Bravo speaks very forcefully on all of this in *Jesús, hombre en conflicto*, 70–71, 300.

9. I am thankful to L. Mosconi for his powerful insights on membership in the Kingdom in *Evangelho de Jesus Cristo segundo Marcos* (São Paulo: Loyola, 1997), 79–93.

10. When we moderns think of "leprosy" we usually think of the very debilitating condition called Hansen's disease. This is clearly not meant in the OT because there "leprosy" refers to any unusual condition of discoloring of human skin, people's clothes, and even mildew on buildings!

11. Once again, I am deeply indebted to the insights of Carlos Bravo on this pericope (*Jesus, hombre en conflicto*, 79–82).

12. D. Neufeld, "Jesus' Eating Transgressions and Social Impropriety in the Gospel of Mark: A Social Scientific Approach," *BTB* 30 (2000): 20. This article is an excellent description of the theme of food and eating in the Gospel of Mark, occasions where Jesus confronted his opponents and showed that the demands for holiness and honor in the Kingdom of God were quite different from those of the religious leadership of Judaism in his day.

13. Again I am indebted to the fine article of Neufeld on the social dimensions of eating— and in this case of not eating! (ibid., 21).

14. By the name "the Herodians" Mark indicates the aristocratic supporters of King Herod Antipas, the tyrant who will have John the Baptist put to death.

15. See John Meier on this point in his "The Circle of the Twelve: Did It Exist during Jesus' Public Ministry?" (*JBL* 116 [1997]: 635). For a less technical presentation of the ministry of the Twelve see Meier's "Are There Historical Links between the Historical Jesus and the Christian Ministry?" in *Theology Digest* 47 (2001): 302–15.

16. Carlos Mesters expands on this idea of sharing as the necessary mode of living in his article, "Jesus e a cultura do seu povo" ("Jesus and the Culture of His People," *EstBíb* 61 [1999]: esp. 19–20).

17. 2:17–22; 3:24–27; 4:21–25; 7:15, 28–29; 9:50; 13:28–29, 33–37; the two similitudes ("The Kingdom of God is like . . .") are in 4:26–29 and 30–32.

18. In the Old Testament the image of a bridegroom is not used for any "messianic" figure, but it is used of God in Isa 62:5 (cf. Isa 54:4–8; Ezek 16:8–14; Hos 2:19). This OT allusion again underlines the presence of God in the Kingdom ministry of Jesus.

19. Mesters, *Caminhamos ná estrada de Jesus: o evangelho de Marcos* (National Conference of Brazilian Bishops; São Paulo: Paulinas, 1996), 121. This is clearly the will of God, Mesters continues, since Deut 15:4 says, "There should be no one of you in need."

20. This insight is from the powerful conclusion of João Inácio Wenzel's book, *Pedagogia de Jesus segundo Marcos* (São Paulo: Ed. Paulinas, 1997), 162.

21. Xabier Pikaza, *Pan, casa, palabra: La iglesia en Marcos* (Biblioteca des estudios bíblicos 94; Salamanca: Sigueme, 1998), 107. Also see Rafael Aguirre's excellent essay on the Kingdom of God in *La mesa compartida: Estudios del NT desde las ciencias sociales* (Presencia teologica 77; Santander: Sal Terrae, 1994), 135–63.

22. This description of Jesus' activity in Part 2 of the Gospel is more fully delineated by Carlos Bravo in his article "Jesus de Nazaret, el Cristo liberador" in *Mysterium liberationis: Conceptos fundamentales de la teología de la liberation* (2nd ed.; Madrid: Ed. Trotta, 1994), 1:551–73, esp. 564–66.

23. See Bruce J. Malina and Richard L. Rohrbaugh, *Social-Science: Commentary on the Synoptic Gospels* (2nd ed.; Minneapolis: Fortress, 2000), 419–20, for a full description of this traditional Mediterranean way of thinking.

24. The unmodified word "life" *(zōē)* occurs elsewhere throughout the NT for the kind of life one can have in relationship with God *now*, e.g., "How narrow . . . the road that leads to life" (Matt 7:14); "One's life does not consist of possessions" (Luke 12:15); and very often in the Gospel according to John.

25. To add to their powerlessness in ancient times, children were extremely vulnerable to disease and other misfortune. Thirty percent of those who were born alive (30% died in childbirth!) died by the age of six and another 30 percent by age sixteen. See Malina and Rohrbaugh, *Social-Science Commentary on the Synoptic Gospels.* Here we cite the article on children on p. 336.

26. Lawful inheritance of such ill-gotten gain does not justify how it was acquired. Since economic stability was almost always based on the ownership of land, the monopoly of the land by the rich kept the poor in a continual state of subjection and dependence on the whims of the landed.

27. Cook and Foulkes, *Marcos,* 277.

28. Once again we are beholden to Carlos Bravo for this powerful insight (*Jesús, hombre en conflicto,* 300).

29. See Carlos Bravo's full explanation of the Last Supper in his *Jesús, hombre en conflicto,* 220–21. Also very noteworthy is that of Carlos Mesters (*Caminhamos na estrada de Jesus,* 75).

30. See Francis J. Moloney, *The Gospel of Mark: A Commentary* (Peabody, Mass.: Hendrickson, 2002), 286.

31. Morna Hooker hints at this conclusion in her Black's New Testament Commentary, *The Gospel according to Saint Mark* (Peabody, Mass.: Hendrickson, 1991), 343.

32. In what follows I am indebted to the excellent commentary of Sharyn Dowd, *Reading Mark: A Literary and Theological Commentary on the Second Gospel* (Reading the New Testament; Macon, Ga.: Smyth & Helwys, 2000), 164–65.

33. This is indeed what happens in the conclusion to the Gospel of Matthew (28:16–20), where the disciples encounter the Risen Jesus on a mountain in Galilee.

34. My thanks to Luis Mosconi for his excellent meditation on the freedom and confidence of Jesus in his *Evangelho de Jesus Cristo segundo Marcos,* 73–75.

35. Thanks to Johan Konings (*Marcos,* 66) and Carlos Bravo (*Jesus, hombre en conflicto,* 297, 301) for this interpretive key to the Gospel as a whole.

36. We can compare St. Paul's use of the phrase "in power" in connection with the resurrection in Rom 1:4—Christ Jesus was "established as Son of God in power according to the spirit of holiness through the resurrection."

37. Hugh Humphrey discusses "the Kingdom come in power," the dramatic reversal of the weakness of the disciples and their enablement to preach the Kingdom because of the resurrection in his excellent book, *He Is Risen! A New Reading of Mark's Gospel* (New York: Paulist, 1992), 153–56.

38. Juan Mateos and Fernando Camacho, *Marcos: Texto y Comentario* (Córdoba, Spain: El Almendro, 1994), 248. Although the original Gospel of Mark does not portray the resurrected Jesus eating and drinking with the disciples, the witness of St. Paul shows that the eucharistic meal was well established in the Christian church already in the 50s (1 Cor 11:23–34). Mark clearly alludes to this practice in his presentation of the Miraculous Feedings (6:30–44 and 8:1–9). The tradition after Mark also records a meal in which Jesus "took bread, said the blessing, broke it, and gave it to [his disciples]" after his resurrection (Luke 24:30; cf. the postresurrection meals with Jesus in the Longer Ending of Mark [16:14] and in John 21:9–13).

39. As is well known, when Matthew calls it "the Kingdom of Heaven" he is merely following the Jewish custom of avoidance of the divine name of God. Out of reverence he substitutes the word "heaven," the place where God dwells, for "God."

40. Mateos and Camacho, *Marcos,* 78.

41. On this important conclusion see Bravo, *Jesús, hombre en conflicto,* 69–70.

PART II

The Eschatology of Mark's Gospel

—4—
CULTURAL CONSIDERATIONS IN ANCIENT THINKING

INTRODUCTION:
THE APOCALYPTIC GENRE

The Hebrew Bible (the Old Testament) is a record of the revelation of God over many centuries to the people God chose to bring salvation to the world. It deals with the origins of that people, going back to creation itself to explain human nature and the reasons why humanity needs God's saving help. The Bible also records the development of the nation of Israel, its many wonderful accomplishments, and its sinful lapses from God's plan. Finally, it tells of God's promises to save the whole world through the mediation of the Chosen People and the savior that God will raise up from them. This last theme is called eschatology, because it foretells what the *final* interventions of God will be in history for the world's salvation. The most prominent kinds of eschatology in the Old Testament are that of the prophets both before and after the Babylonian Exile, and that of a later kind of Jewish writing called "apocalyptic."

Apocalyptic eschatology predicts a sudden "revelation" (Greek *apocalypsis* means "revelation"). In it God's infinite power bursts into the world to end the evils of history and make things right for humanity. In ancient Judaism a whole genre of literature concerned this kind of eschatology, examples of which are the Book of Daniel in the Old Testament and a whole raft of later Jewish texts like the Books of *Enoch, Jubilees, 4 Ezra,* and the Qumran War and Temple Scrolls among the Dead Sea Scrolls. The Book of Revelation is the only fully apocalyptic text in the New Testament, but a number of apocalypses were written later in the early church.

The Gospel of Mark, however, is not itself an apocalypse. In fact, it has much more in common with the ancient *"Life of"* (*bios* in Greek) genre of

Hellenistic literature. Yet that is not a perfect description of it either. The Gospel was not written in the high literary style of, say, Plutarch's *Parallel Lives,* and it has important differences in content. It is really rather like ancient novelistic literature, like the romances that were read aloud for the enjoyment of the common people who couldn't read themselves. Like them, the Gospel of Mark is characterized by foreshadowings of what is to come later in the narrative, echoes of earlier stories, repetitions of key words and phrases, and presentations of similar stories, all woven together to "keep the audience on track as to where the story has been and where it is going."[1] Of course, the Gospel of Mark is not a novel or a romance, but a narrative that combines several features of ancient writing.

While it shares some characteristics of Hellenistic literature, the Gospel of Mark is very Jewish, since it practically takes the Old Testament as its blueprint and tells the life of a very Jewish Messiah. It shares a lot with the prophetic eschatology of the writings of the Book of Isaiah, especially in its descriptions of the restorative miracles of Jesus, his death as the Suffering Servant, and its call "to faithfulness and transformation" in expectation of the fulfillment of Jesus' promises.[2] And yet it also shares much of the language of Jewish apocalyptic, its images, and even its main point of view, namely that God's power will suddenly manifest itself (in the coming of the Son of Man) for the salvation of the world. Mark differs from the strictly Jewish apocalyptic genre, however, in that the Gospel is mainly about the *past* events of Jesus' life, except in the Discourse of chapter 13 and a few other sayings of Jesus. Another big difference is that in Jewish apocalyptic, salvation, the coming of the Spirit of God, and the renewal of the world are purely future events, while in Mark these ultimate events have already begun. Thus we can say that although the Gospel of Mark is not an apocalypse, its author has chosen to use apocalyptic thinking and language in his presentation of the message of Jesus Christ and the program for action for his followers in Mark's church.

Before studying the eschatology of the Gospel of Mark, it is crucial to clarify some aspects of the apocalyptic language he uses in his presentation of Jesus' urgent message for the future, specifically those that are understood differently by cultures other than our own: symbolic language, the perception of time, and the self-identification of the human person within the community.

THE SYMBOLIC VALUE OF APOCALYPTIC LANGUAGE

The purpose of apocalyptic literature was for the author to use the divine authority of an otherworldly revealer, like the angel in the Book of Daniel or Jesus himself in the Book of Revelation, to exhort or console a group in crisis.

In apocalyptic literature the strength of human imagination is used to construct a symbolic world in which the hopes and values of faith can be upheld in spite of powerlessness and even the threat of death.[3] A mythological picture is created, a symbolic world that transfigures the present, "subverting confidence in the everydayness of existence and buttressing a vision of rich and empowered existence based on the instruction of [an otherworldly revealer]."[4] When historical and social reality cannot be stated in immediate and realistic terms, only the imaginative language of faith can *tell the truth* by a kind of wisdom for understanding the real potential and liabilities of the situation.

The mode of communication of apocalyptic is symbolic: it relates that which cannot be perceived by abstract concepts by encoding and transmitting a fuller, psychic, experience. According to philosopher Herbert Musurillo, apocalyptic language is "almost pre-logical, as though it were a vast mosaic or a musical cult hymn."[5] It arouses a deep emotional experience, "releases hidden energies in the soul," and communicates levels of meaning not accessible through immediate experience or conceptual thought.[6] Mexican writer Virgil Elizondo relates his experience of a pilgrimage group at the shrine of Our Lady of Guadalupe in such symbolic language. "It was as if we were all entering together into the common womb of the Americas," he says. "I needed no explanation for my experience. I had lived it. In that sacred space, I was part of the communion of earth and heaven, of present family and ancestors, and of generations to come. It became one of the core moments of my life."[7] The symbolic language of apocalyptic is like "a work of art—like some grand painting which *moves* the reader from feelings of disappointment and despair to feelings of great strength, courage, fearlessness and hope."[8]

In the corpus of ancient apocalyptic writing almost every cosmic and terrestrial element has an assigned symbolic value. For example, the darkened sun is a supernatural sign of the arrival of the presence of the Lord God, whether in Amos 8:9, Jer 15:9, Mark 13:24, or at the crucifixion of Jesus in Mark 15:33. By the first century "a tradition of symbolism" in Judaism made apocalyptic literature decipherable by everyone.[9] These symbols, which were "the codes and raw materials of apocalyptic,"[10] derived their religious significance from the oracles of late OT prophecy, "a background of thought in which they had already served as symbols for religious conceptions."[11] Thus the same OT image of falling stars (Isa 34:4) by which Isaiah predicted the fall of Edom can be used by Mark in 13:25 and by John of Patmos in the Book of Revelation 6:13 to describe the cosmic stage to be set for the triumph of the Son of Man and the Lamb, respectively.

Such an approach to symbol is natural to many Latin American readers of the Gospels. They, unlike us, have no need of the foregoing explanation but intuit the meaning of biblical symbols because "they interpret the events of their own lives in exactly the same way."[12] This point is very important for our interpretation of the Gospel of Mark: the most meaningful and personal experiences of the people are understood and expressed most powerfully by symbolic language. For us post-Enlightenment thinkers, the most gripping language is *abstract,* like the description of Jesus' life as a *Proexistenz* (we especially like the density of German abstract terms), which means a life or existence totally dedicated "for" (*pro* in Latin) others. Mark likes to show the very same idea by Jesus' *symbolic* language, in which he likens his life (concretely his body and his blood) to the sacrificial offering of a lamb to God in the Old Testament. I myself am excited by an abstract phrase such as "tensive language," used by Norman Perrin to indicate that the symbolic language of the parables holds several meanings in tension and is not capable of being completely captured by any single explanation.[13] Jesus preferred just to tell the story.

Mark brings the same excitement to the reader by actually using the parable of the Fig Tree in the Eschatological Discourse (chap. 13). He lets the parable's concrete language do the work of bringing together in a single symbol such varied realities as the destruction of the Temple, the blossoming of the church as the new house of God, *and* the Coming of the Son of Man.

A very good example of this concrete yet multilayered thinking in Latin America is the Nahuatl saga, the *Nican Mopohua.* Here is a powerful expression of the validity of Christianity as fulfilling the people's native religiosity. In the miraculous image of Our Lady of Guadalupe on the garment of the Indian peasant Juan Diego, she appears surrounded by the sun. She blocks its violent rays from harming the viewer, just as she blocks the terrible blood worship of the Aztec sun god. Yet she doesn't destroy this "the true God, Téotl," but claims that she is his mother. She appears standing on the moon, just as Earth Mother subdued Moon in Aztec mythology, after Moon had vowed to do away with Sun, of whom she was jealous, and bring eternal darkness upon the earth. On and on the symbols go, from the blue and green colors of her cloak (the colors of sky and earth) to the flowers she produced in the midst of winter to show her commitment to health and healing.

One must conclude, then, that apocalyptic thinking does not follow the principles of "Western logic," that it is "expressive rather than referential, symbolic rather than factual."[14] Its language is employed to move to action or to console rather than to describe ontological reality.[15] And so the images used are not to be taken literally, as so many North Atlantic scholars mistakenly try to do, imagining that apocalyptic texts refer to some cosmic, physical catastrophe, when they are meant to convey meaning in a referential way. They point to a salvific, *terrestrial* future by projecting a completely symbolic *celestial* universe.[16] In this two-level picture of reality, God guarantees that what happens in the heavenly sphere will come to pass just the same on the earthly stage of life. The heavenly events "slightly precede [the earthly events] in time, leading them into existence, so to speak," and are often called the "things to come."[17] Thus Jesus, whose heavenly reality in glory was glimpsed already at the Transfiguration, will surely receive that glory from God in order to come and "gather [his] elect from the four winds" (13:27). The true identity of Jesus is that he, as the celestial "Son of Man has authority to forgive sins *on earth*" (2:10).

This thinking in symbols explains a phenomenon in Mark that has puzzled many interpreters of the Gospels. Mark's richness and creativity as an author have only recently come to the fore because his language and style have been considered "clumsy" because of his frequent redundancy, repetition, and lack of logical order. The general consensus was that Mark was untrained as a writer and not very clever either. Yet recent literary criticism has shown that his writing is replete with symbolism, often carried out through the whole Gospel with vibrant reverberations of Jesus' life and death as a new Exodus.[18] Motifs of baptism, temptation, the "strong man," the celestial Son of Man, the Suffering Righteous One of the Book of Wisdom, and many more permeate the text from its initial chapters to its mysterious ending in 16:8.

How can it be that a person so obviously untrained in the subtleties of Hellenistic writing was so skilled at weaving together such a forceful presentation of Jesus? How is it that Mark so powerfully draws the reader forward in the story? Mark, like many ancients (and like many Latin Americans), *thought* in symbol. He processed reality and gained a profound understanding of it by conceiving its meaning symbolically. Thus Mark, instead of taking the historical fact of Jesus' baptism by John in the Jordan, and seeing it as a literary motif that can also describe his suffering and death, understood the Passion as a washing, a flushing away of the limitations of human love. It was as the one truly pure sacrifice God wanted for the salvation of the world that Jesus underwent such affliction and humiliation. For Mark, Jesus was also the "strong man" who could easily defeat Satan in his many exorcisms. The "power" of the aristocratic priesthood was no match for the power of him who courageously endured unrighteous execution to unmask their corruption and hypocrisy forever. Mark's thought processes were symbolical, and that is the key to unlocking the mystery of how he presents Jesus' confident prediction of the future—Jesus' urgent message for today.

ORIENTATION TO AND EXPERIENCE OF TIME

One of our biggest problems in dealing with the eschatological texts of the New Testament is the way we North Atlantic people think about time. In a recent conceptual presentation of temporality in the Bible, Bruce Malina maintains that much of what contemporary biblical scholarship takes as referring to the future is really about what should be understood as defining the present.[19] He claims that modern readers of the Bible need to understand the profound difference between our modern, quantitative concept of time and the ancient perception of time, which is oriented to present experience. If we do not see the difference, we will forever be locked into a point of view that puts the fulfillment of Jesus' words ever farther into the future. In fact, for many of us the glorious future promised in the New Testament has receded into oblivion.

What follows will be a re-presentation of Malina's ideas on time and culture in a less technical manner, to which will be added some new insights and examples from personal experience. First of all, let us examine the way we, in modern societies, think about time. For us, Malina points out, time is like a ribbon that stretches in a straight line from the past into the future. Along its path, one's life unfolds in equal, measurable units: minutes, hours, days, years. Because such a conception of time is very useful for planning and controlling reality, the inevitable result is that the lives of most middle-class North Atlantic individuals are oriented toward some future goal(s). This, we think, is good, and perhaps the main asset to our "getting things done," so that we can be successful in controlling and gaining an ever firmer hold on material reality.

A classic statement of this attitude is given by Ayn Rand, American "Objectivist" philosopher, in one of the many diatribes of Dagny Taggert, a character in her novel *Atlas Shrugged:*

> It is not proper for a man's life to be a circle . . . or a string of circles dropping off like zeros behind him—man's life must be a straight line of motion from goal to farther goal, each leading to the next and to a single growing sum, like a journey down the track of a railroad, from station to station.[20]

To this way of thinking, the present is to be spent in a way to position ourselves better in a calculated future, and the past is unrecoverable. Therefore, anything that has not contributed to progress up to this moment is considered forfeit, just as any present nongoal-oriented activity is just "wasting time." All well and good. We are, in fact, very successful in producing things "on time" and in accumulating an enormous bounty of material goods.

The fact of the matter, however, is that most of the world's people now, and the vast majority of people who have ever lived on the planet, experience time very differently. Most "Two-Thirds World" societies even today, and certainly the ancient Circum-Mediterraneans who wrote the Bible, were/are temporally oriented to the present, and not to the future as we are. Unlike moderns, the ancients did not conceive of time as an abstract, quantifiable, and fleeting entity, but as the duration of the *present.* They regarded time as one long *now,* one might say, with its "immediate future bound up with the present as well as previous activity still resonating in the present."[21] Of course, they could think about past and future happenings, but only as related in some way to present experience, like the ordeal of healing from a broken leg, where the past is still vivid in the mind and a future return to regular activity is forthcoming, or as in the experience of expecting a baby, when so much of what is forthcoming is experienced in some way as actually present.

In such a culture people simply do not think about the future in any abstract way. Their perception of time has "no reference to future possibility or probability, only to what was going to be and must be because it already is."[22] In fact, for first-century Jews and Christians, the unpredictable future was in no way a matter of strategic planning, but the exclusive domain of God, as Jesus affirms in the Marcan Eschatological Discourse, "But of that day or hour, no one knows, . . . only the Father" (13:32).

As an example of this cultural phenomenon of a present orientation to time, I'd like to tell you about the ordination of my friend, David (pronounce it "Da-*veed*"). Although David was a student here at our seminary for some four years and was being ordained for a U.S. diocese, his bishop kindly agreed to ordain him to the priesthood in his hometown in Mexico. I asked David if I might join the festivities and if he could find me a place to stay for a few days to visit. He said that he would be delighted and that accommodations would not be a problem. A week and a half before the ordination, I tried to contact David to finalize the details of my visit, having already procured my plane tickets. I finally tracked him down through email to an American colleague of his, who was studying Spanish and staying with David's family there and thus in contact with him. David sent a quick email note thanking me profusely for my promise to come and said, "I will write to you next week. I am on retreat until Wednesday, so I will email you then." The ordination itself was to be only two days after that!

I had to start my journey early in order to stop in Atlanta for another ordination the weekend before the one in Mexico, so I couldn't wait for his reply. I phoned David's mother to say that I would meet everyone at the cathedral on the day of the ordination and made arrangements with some other friends to be picked up at the airport in Mexico. Those friends are German, and so they confirmed everything at once and were there at the airport to pick me up on time—of course!

When we got to the cathedral, David was out in the plaza having pictures taken with the bishop. I waited until they were finished and went up to him, suitcase in hand. He gave me a warm welcome and said, "Go with my sister to the reception after the ceremony." I didn't know which sister he meant, but David was hurrying away, saying that he was late for his own ordination.

I managed to find the right sister and went with her and her family to the reception. At the reception, after a great dinner and some wonderful entertainment, I was almost completely frantic, wondering what I (and my suitcase out in the foyer) was going to do that night. David eventually came and took me over to another table to meet the family he had evidently just asked to put me up for the next couple of days. It was after ten o'clock at night!

When I met the family, they were absolutely charming. Indeed, they were thrilled to have me come to their house, and we had a wonderful visit for several days. You see, there was no need for me to worry. Celebrating the ordination of David was what they were *doing* that weekend—all five hundred of the invited guests. There were probably twenty-five families that would have been happy to put me up that night!

All this is to point out that people in some other cultures don't plan out all the details of a future visit like we do. They *can't,* I don't think, just as Malina says, because they *do not think* concretely about the merely possible future. Something like that they will deal with "*mañana.*" With regard to my visit to David, he didn't make detailed plans for my stay because he was completely involved with what he was doing at the moment, his ordination retreat. Once I actually arrived at the cathedral, however, he easily dealt with that concrete reality, because here everyone was focused on *that* present moment, and nothing else.

So now, back to our question of the perception of time in the Gospel of Mark. In his article, Malina goes on to say that when the earliest Christians experienced the presence of the resurrected Jesus, these enthusiastic disciples basked in a kind of euphoria since all of his promises seemed on the brink of fulfillment. Later on, however, when persecution came upon the early churches, the promised Kingdom of God, Jesus' coming as Messiah with power, and a change of fortune for God's people were all *no longer* linked to the experiential present in any obvious way. Indeed, it looked like all was lost.

For the present-oriented early Christians this change in outlook had serious and negative results. A belief in what was only *possible* could not sustain them, because in their cultural mindset present action could only be based on what was clearly comprehensible as *forthcoming* in their perception of reality. As Malina puts it, "it would be foolhardy in the extreme to make decisions for the world of experience on the basis of the imaginary and its past and/or future."[23] Thus, for example, there would have been a great temptation for the early Christian communities in Palestine to join the Jewish rebellion against Rome, as a much more apparently forthcoming solution to their present situation. To continue to place confidence in some now unforeseeable power of Jesus Christ to change the situation was unthinkable without some other guarantee. We can see the result of this crisis in Mark 13, in the stern warnings to flee Judea and not to listen to the promises of such false messiahs.

In Malina's technical language, what Jesus promised was shifted out of their experienced time and projected into "imaginary time," or what I prefer to call "imagination time," since the former appellation may imply that such time does not concern reality. "Imagination time" includes *whatever* can be thought of but that falls *outside* the horizon of the experienced world, much as we moderns might say is the *merely possible*. For the ancients, whatever is not oriented to present experience can make no difference in their lives.

Mark found the solution to the crisis of the persecution of his early church and the destruction of the Temple in the apocalyptic traditions attributed to Jesus. Here is how apocalyptic works: while experienced time was normally validated only by sensory experience—seeing, touching, or hearing (e.g., Mark 16:6: "Behold the place where they laid him")—events outside concrete experience could only be assured by the testimony of a credible person.[24] Because of this, the *reality* promised in imagination time could be proclaimed and validated, too, by a reliable witness acting in the divine sphere as, for example, the OT prophet knows what God wills for future history in Jer 31:31–34. This divine assurance, in fact, is the reason for apocalyptic discourse: the otherworldy figure—in the case of the Gospels and the Book of Revelation Jesus himself—guarantees what is to be because he belongs to the celestial sphere. Mark's Jesus says, "The kingdom of God is at hand" (1:15), because he perceives its effects as already present in his life. With regard to the future arrival of the end of persecution and final reunion with him in glory, the enthroned Jesus of the Book of Revelation (and of Mark 13) guarantees them because they are already accomplished in the heavenly sphere of reality.

One cannot emphasize enough, however, that imagination time is still oriented to the present; that is, it is apprehended so as to make a difference in *present* attitude and behavior. Even expectations validated by Jesus himself could not be projected into some *set point* in the future, as Mark's Jesus says, "But of that day or hour, no one knows . . . only the Father" (13:32), since the absolute future is the realm of God alone. Thus if Jesus' promises were to have any meaning for the future of Mark's community, they had to make a real difference in how the community saw itself and acted *now*.

How, then, would the earliest Christians have apprehended Jesus' marvelous prediction of God's salvific solution to human suffering? The answer is in Jesus' central teaching about the Kingdom of God. The Kingdom represents the definitive plan of God that will come to pass because it already is: "The kingdom of God is at hand" (Mark 1:15). The ancients could not give up their orientation to present experience and thus had to affirm their trust in the words of Jesus about the future by means of concrete present activity.

The actual mechanism by which the early Christians could live in anticipation of the final coming of Christ is a bit difficult for us North Atlantic types to understand. As Malina points out, anthropologists have found that in nonmodern societies time concepts are determined more by structural (social) interrelations and by the set procedures of farming and husbandry than by some kind of autonomous clock time as in our modern societies. We could take as an illustration a classic study of the Nuer people of Africa, in which cultural anthropologist E. E. Evans-Pritchard observed this kind of "procedural time" and explained it thoroughly.[25] Instead, we have decided to illustrate this experience of "imagination time" by a description of the festival of Carnaval in Brazil, an unforgettable happening I experienced in February of 1997. Carnaval (the Brazilian Portuguese name for what we call Mardi Gras) is truly a mythological time. It occurs over the weekend before Ash Wednesday and is a time of total abandon of mundane cares and normal lifestyles. All year long the Brazilians prepare for it, many of them making costumes and practicing the new music written for the upcoming festival. These songs are well known by the time the festival arrives, because they are Top Ten popular hits as soon as they are written. However, the actual celebration of Carnaval does not begin until the Friday before Ash Wednesday, a date set by the (divine authority of the) Church each year.

To explain how different a time Carnaval is in the lives of normal Brazilians, let me share my experience. Saturday is the night for the big parades we always see on television, and in São Paulo they take place in the Sambadromo, a kind of huge hippodrome or racetrack. A huge avenue runs down the middle, flanked on both sides by stands for the 100,000-plus spectators lucky enough to get tickets for the evening. We arrived at about nine-thirty to see some four to five thousand marvelously costumed dancers and musicians parade by, everyone dancing to the contagious rhythms of the samba tunes. I was amazed at my friends' ability to dance on and on while I had to sit down and rest frequently. At four-thirty in the morning the last escola passed by and we were all tired and hungry. I asked a friend if we could go to breakfast at such an hour. He simply said, "This is São Paulo!" By the time we got back to the monastery where I was staying it was a quarter to eight in the morning, almost time for Sunday Mass. I put on my religious habit and went to church. At the kiss of peace, when I greeted my neighbor, saying, "A paz de Cristo," and bowed, confetti fell out of my hair!

In the Bible something divinely guaranteed as forthcoming could actually come about only when the time was right, when God alone judged it "time." The divine guarantee, however, could begin the change of lifestyle demanded by God's spokesperson, as, for example, the promise of divine punishment brings about the repentance of the Assyrians in the biblical Book of Jonah. New Testament apocalyptic eschatology, then, is best understood as the course of history revealed as the running of a predefined (by God) course of events, in a kind of procedural time. As the Hebrew people became oppressed in the past by the Egyptians, the Philistines, the Babylonians, and so on, God raised up each time a savior for the people who led them to turn to rely on God's effective power. For this reason, the apocalyptic vision uses many allusions to the biblical record of God's past interventions to prove a kind of procedure in which the future is assured by calling to mind the past, where God's journey had begun. In this way the apocalyptic seer can open up the future and lead the people to comprehend and welcome God's new interventions, God's eschatological *kairoi.*[26] The apocalyptic seer recounts the various stages up to the present point as predicted by God, identifies the present as part of the plan, and then goes on to affirm the final stages that are yet to come.

Carlos Mesters has used a graphic metaphor to explain this aspect of apocalyptic thinking.[27] Imagine a long bus journey through an underdeveloped part of Brazil. The passengers need reassurance to continue on the journey through the dark night of many detours and difficult roads. The bus driver, who is familiar with the region, explains to the passengers in detail what part of the journey has already transpired. He tells them where they are now and reassures them that they are on course by informing them about what legs of the journey lie ahead before they arrive at their proper destination. So also, as we shall see, in the Eschatological Discourse the Evangelist Mark has Jesus describe what has already happened to the early Christians in order to assure them of the future.

The hopeful images of NT apocalyptic were part of an imagination-time, forthcoming world described by the early Christian prophets and apocalyptic visionaries who built on Jesus' teaching on the Kingdom of God. They knew that it had broken into human experience again and again in Jesus' lifetime and that its definitive arrival was guaranteed by his own words. The Kingdom is thus always forthcoming, and the End of this time period of the world is just waiting for God to make it happen. Rather than fear the next stage of history in God's eschatological timeline, Christians were exhorted to be ready for it and even to cooperate in bringing it about.

In summary, then, the early Christians apprehended the Eschaton as something continually just over the horizon, something in which they could participate in an anticipatory way, something they expected to unfold itself completely *at any moment,* depending on when God so willed it. Indeed, the eschatological Kingdom of God was constantly breaking in upon them, in the miraculous spread of the gospel to foreign lands, in the many healings and exorcisms of the apostolic mission, in the downfall of every tyrant who oppressed the early church. God would/will bring it about fully just as soon as God wills it.

HUMAN SELF-IDENTITY

This brings us to our third point of cultural difference: the ancient collectivistic self-identity versus our modern individualism. The embeddedness of the ancient person in society is a sociological factor so different from our modern psychological independence that without grasping it we cannot appreciate the self-awareness of the early Christians. Their different understanding of the imperatives of biblical moral teaching stands in striking contrast to that of most of us moderns. Of all North Atlantic people, Americans especially are convinced that the Bible is concerned mainly with the quality of life of the individual, and that sin is defined only as the actions for which one is personally responsible. Our incredible prosperity is seen as having no relation to, or responsibility for, the dire poverty and ignorance of so much of the world's population. Perhaps there is no perspective in the Bible that is more radically different from the way we perceive ourselves and our relationship to society.

Bruce Malina has published a very fine explanation of the difference between the modern individualistic conception of the human being as "person" and the ancient Mediterranean societies' notion of the human-as-group-member.[28] He points out that the ancients did not think at all about humans as individuals, and that, in fact, the Greeks did not even have a word for "person." All thinking was geared to people as members of their *group* and not to their particular characteristics or limitations. Thus there was never any question of what was morally required of an individual. Every personal decision was dictated by one's position in family, village, or larger group, and there was never a case of the agony of an individual not knowing which alternative behavior to choose. All thinking was geared to people as *group* members, where all possible responses to any situation were divisible in two: one either *did* or *did not* carry out one's preordained role in the community to which one belonged.[29]

To illustrate the reality of this social embeddedness with an example once again from Latin America, let me tell you the story of my Brazilian friend Henrique. When I met Henrique at our priory in Vinhedo, he was a young student in dental school. We had several excellent conversations about religion, the church, and the message of Jesus Christ for today. I knew Henrique was very pleased with our meetings when, a few days before I was scheduled to leave, he brought a *lembrança* to the monastery for me. The Brazilians have a beautiful custom of offering to people they visit a little memento (*lembrança* in Portuguese). It was a very nice, hand-embroidered towel, with my difficult name spelled correctly. Accompanying the present was a note of profound appreciation in flowery Portuguese, although we had always spoken in the English he had mastered so well. Below his signature were the signatures of his father, his mother, and his sister. My attention to this young student was seen as an honor to the whole family. Can you imagine a twenty-one-year-old American letting his parents and sister even see such a letter, much less asking them to sign it? Yet the behavior of Henrique and his family would be the natural thing for an ancient Circum-Mediterranean person to do as well.

A good description of this self-perception of the "collectivistic personality" is Virgil Elizondo's record of his pilgrimage at six years of age to the shrine of Our Lady of Guadalupe in Mexico:

> We finally arrived at the basilica in rhythmic procession with the thousands of others who moved, it seemed, as one collective body. When we entered through the huge doors . . . it was as if we were all entering into the common womb of the Americas. . . . We could not stop; the crowd simply moved us on. We were never pushed or shoved; we all simply walked in deep mystical union with one another. We were in the rhythmic movement of the universe—indeed, at this moment we were in contact with the very source of life and movement.[30]

A second set of differences between the modern U.S. and the Circum-Mediterranean personality in Malina's presentation is in one's perception of external reality and the control one may have over one's life. Simplifying the language of the Culture Personality School of anthropology that Malina uses, we can say that the ancients understood the conditions of the world as not of their making, but as the result of political, religious, economic, and kinship forces—a realistic enough picture of reality. The problem with many of them, however, was that they also believed that they were not at all in control of their lives. They felt powerless to act freely, seeing themselves as totally controlled by outside agencies such as cosmic forces, deities, luck, and fate.

What Jesus and the Christian movement tried to accomplish, according to this schema, was to bring about in believers a change in that predicament. People, with God's help, can exercise more mastery over their own lives by becoming members of the Christian family. With the rite of baptism and their commitment to do God's will, they transfer their identity to a group whose moral and spiritual freedom were the immediate result of God's grace. At the same time they retain their realistic acknowledgment of the deficiencies of the external world, that "enduring problems [in society] point to something wrong with the system or with the situation."[31] The perfect biblical example of such a newfound freedom is that of Psalm 131:2: "Like a *weaned* child on its mother's lap, / so is my soul within me." Since the child has been weaned, it may take the initiative to drink or not, but the nourishment of life must still be provided from the bounty of the mother.[32] When Jesus casts out the demon with these words, "Quiet! Come out of him" (Mark 1:25), he restores the power to control his life to the possessed man.

How *different* is the dominant cultural personality of modern times with its rugged individualism in which "the individual believes he/she is in control of life *and* is basically responsible for whatever happens, for good or for ill."[33] This self-perception brings about two rather unhealthy results. First, the individual turns inward and comes to believe in an unrealistic autonomy, often with dire results.

> Western cultures, which place a premium on self-reliance, achievement, and power and control over life, nature and others, all focus on these factors internal to the individual as decisive and necessary. The individual, however, is held accountable for whatever occurs, so frustrated goals mean a lack of ability, and failure evokes self-blame, guilt, depression, and feelings of inadequacy.[34]

Just look at how many self-help and how-to-succeed books line the shelves of our bookstores! Commencement speakers tell the graduating class "You can be anything you want to be!" and thus help to set them up for a life of tragic disappointment.

Second, this configuration of perceived responsibility may cause individualists to give up on the world beyond their immediate grasp, with the determinist's apology that everything exterior to oneself happens because of "nature or nurture." One turns toward the self as the main project of a human life and begins to think that nothing can be done to change the gross inequities in our world. We despair of helping the exploited in developing countries because they are not, like us, taking charge of their lives.

A more biblical viewpoint, although not necessarily denying to us moderns our concern for our own salvation, will help us to a better appreciation of the communal dynamic in NT eschatology. The ancient Christians understood that we receive salvation as members of a group of believers, because we are defined by them, and not by our individuality. They understood that we are responsible for helping the less fortunate—the poor, the infirm, the spiritually handicapped—to participate in a life of peace and justice. They heard the Gospel accounts of the compassion of Jesus, his outrage at the oppression of people by forces beyond their control. A proper reading of the biblical text today mandates that we, too, must be concerned with the lives of our brothers and sisters everywhere, especially where dehumanizing factors are rampant. This, for Mark, becomes the central concern of the Church, the new family of God, whose main task is the spread of the gospel, that is, of Jesus' message of justice and freedom.

NOTES

1. See the excellent introduction to the genre of Mark in Sharyn Dowd, *Reading Mark: A Literary and Theological Commentary on the Second Gospel* (Reading the New Testament; Macon, Ga.: Smyth & Helwys, 2000), 2.

2. Again the introduction of Dowd is right on target (see p. 6).

3. John J. Collins, *The Apocalyptic Imagination: An Introduction to Jewish Apocalyptic Literature* (2nd ed.; Grand Rapids: Eerdmans, 1998), 283. Collins says, "The function of the apocalyptic literature is to shape one's imaginative perception of a situation and so lay the basis for whatever course of action it exhorts" (42).

4. Kloppenborg, "Symbolic Eschatology and the Apocalypticism of Q," *HTR* 80 (1987): 304.

5. Herbert Musurillo, *Symbolism in the Christian Imagination* (Baltimore: Helicon, 1962), 28.

6. Avery Dulles, "Symbol in Revelation," *New Catholic Encyclopedia* (New York: McGraw-Hill, 1967), 13:862.

7. Virgil Elizondo, *Guadalupe, Mother of the New Creation* (Maryknoll, N.Y.: Orbis, 1998), x.

8. So Albert Nolan in the foreword to Carlos Mesters, *The Hope of the People Who Struggle: The Key to Reading the Apocalypse of St. John* (Athlone, South Africa: Theology Exchange Program, 1994), ix.

9. Lacoque, "Apocalyptic Symbolism: A Ricoeurian Hermeneutical Approach," *Biblical Research* 26 (1981): 12. According to J. J. Collins, "The vision accounts [of the Book of Daniel] do not derive from the private, subjective consciousness (or subconscious) of an individual. They are formulated in traditional language, much of which is drawn ultimately from ancient Near Eastern mythology" (*The Apocalyptic Vision of the Book of Daniel* [HSM 16; Missoula, Mont.: Scholars Press, 1977], 95). This is an important insight into the ancient manner of thinking with concrete symbols rather than the abstract concepts in which many modern people think. N. Perrin has called apocalyptic symbols "steno-symbols," literary figures immediately exhausted by a one-to-one relationship with their meaning, and so immediately understandable to the ancient reader/hearer ("Eschatology and Hermeneutics: Reflections on Method in the Interpretation of the NT," *JBL* 93 [1974]: 10–11).

10. Collins, *Apocalyptic Imagination*, 22.

11. C. H. Dodd, *The Interpretation of the Fourth Gospel* (Cambridge: University Press, 1954) 137.

12. Mesters, *Defenseless Flower: A New Reading of the Bible* (Maryknoll, N.Y.: Orbis, 1989), 6. The text becomes "a symbol or a mirror of the present situation as the people experience it in community" (ibid., 2).

13. See B. B. Scott's insightful explanation of Perrin and other modern interpreters of kingdom and parable in *Jesus, Symbol-Maker for the Kingdom* (Philadelphia: Fortress, 1981), chap. 1.

14. Collins, *Apocalyptic Imagination*, 17.

15. Ibid., 283. Collins goes on to say that apocalyptic language is "*commissive*," that is, "it commits us to a view of the world for the sake of the actions and attitudes that are entailed."

16. As John L. McKenzie has emphasized, "Crassly literal interpretation of the mythopoeic imagery of eschatology obscures the reality of the divine acts of salvation and judgment" ("Aspects of OT Thought," *The New Jerome Biblical Commentary* [ed. R. E. Brown, J. A. Fitzmyer, and R. E. Murphy; Englewood Cliffs, N.J.: Prentice Hall, 1990], 1313). I can add this note from my own personal experience: Not one Latin American member of any Bible study

group whom I asked about the darkening of the sun and moon in Mark's thirteenth chapter ever referred to it as having a literal meaning that concerned future events that astronomers could record!

17. J. L. Martyn, *History and Theology in the Fourth Gospel* (2nd ed.; Nashville: Abingdon, 1979), 136, cited in the helpful conclusion on the Son of Man in John Ashton, *Understanding the Fourth Gospel* (Oxford: Clarendon, 1991), 368–73.

18. Perhaps the most complete explanation of symbols in the Gospel of Mark is the work of Juan Mateos and Fernando Camacho, *Evangelio, figuras y símbolos* (2nd ed.; Córdoba, Spain: El Almendro, 1992).

19. Malina ("Christ and Time: Swiss or Mediterranean?" *CBQ* 51 [1989]: 9) says, "presumed future-oriented categories of the Bible are in fact not future-oriented at all, but present-oriented."

20. Rand, *Atlas Shrugged* (New York: Signet, 1957), 569–70.

21. Malina, "Christ and Time," 12.

22. Ibid., 16. Thus their perception of reality consisted of "the concrete present with its concrete antecedents and its forthcoming concrete outcomes" (14).

23. Ibid., 16. This is because "the present orientation in the world of experienced time is rooted in experienced disvalue of delayed gratification or anticipatory goal behavior for present survival" (19).

24. Ibid., 16.

25. E. E. Evans-Pritchard, *The Nuer: A Description of the Modes of Livelihood and Political Institutions of a Nilotic People* (Oxford: Clarendon Press, 1940). I recommend the whole chapter on "Time" for some very interesting reading.

26. Xabier Susin (*Assim na terra como no céu: Brevilóquio sobre Escatologia e Criação* [Petrópolis, Brazil: Vozes, 1995], 40) says that the Old Testament *kairoi* demonstrate what is to come yet in the future. They both indicate and determine the direction of even greater future events, acting as a channel to open the future for an even greater intervention of God's power in the covenant relationship. They are a "memory of the future."

27. Mesters, *The Hope of the People Who Struggle,* 28–29.

28. Malina, "Is There a Circum-Mediterranean Person? Looking for Stereotypes," *BTB* 22 (1992): 66–87.

29. B. Malina and J. Neyrey, "First-Century Personality: Dyadic, Not Individualistic," in *The Social World of Luke-Acts* (ed. Jerome Neyrey; Peabody, Mass.: Hendrickson, 1991), 72–83.

30. Elizondo, *Guadalupe,* x.

31. Malina, "Is There a Circum-Mediterranean Person?" 78.

32. Conversation with Rev. Mark Gruber, O.S.B., cultural anthropologist.

33. Malina, "Is There a Circum-Mediterranean Person?" 83 (emphasis added).

34. D. W. Augsburger, *Pastoral Counseling across Cultures* (Philadelphia: Westminster, 1986), 99, as quoted in Malina, "Is There a Circum-Mediterranean Person?" 83.

—5—

ESCHATOLOGY IN
THE GOSPEL OF MARK

Christian apocalyptic differs from its Jewish matrix because for Christians the Messiah has already come, bringing about a new age of history in which the firstfruits of the resurrection are already being enjoyed. Thus there is a palpable presence of Jesus in every suffering Church community, consoling and giving strength in the present time, however much a fuller revelation of God's power is awaited in the (unknowable) future.

My method of presenting Mark's eschatology will be to follow the text of the Gospel in a verse-by-verse examination of the relevant passages, keeping in mind the new understanding of first-century culture as outlined it in the previous chapter.

"THE BEGINNING OF THE GOSPEL"

The first text that we must consider is the first verse of the Gospel, "The beginning of the gospel of Jesus Christ the Son of God." This introductory statement has the grammatical form of a title since there is no predicate in the phrase. With it Mark is identifying his narrative of the public ministry of Jesus as the *beginning* of the "good news," the "gospel" that Jesus asks us to believe in (1:15), so that we may participate in the Kingdom of God even before it fully arrives. Throughout Mark's narrative the message about the Kingdom of God and Jesus' teaching of it by his example point to a *future* in which Jesus' followers will continue what he has started, preaching the gospel "to all nations" (13:10). As we have seen, at the abrupt end of his story, Mark's "young man" calls all who would be disciples of Jesus to go to their own "Galilee," where Jesus will go before them as their shepherd on the way of doing God's will, persevering "to the end" (13:13).

THE EXORCISMS OF JESUS

Immediately after Jesus' baptism by John, Mark shows the apocalyptic character of Jesus' ministry. When Jesus comes up out of the water of the Jordan, the heavens are torn open just as they are in the great apocalyptic prayer of the Book of Isaiah (Isa 63:19b–64:1). There, after the destruction of the first Temple back in the sixth century B.C.E., the prophet prays for God to appear to the nations in power. After the voice of God proclaims Jesus' divine Sonship in Mark 1:11, a whirlwind Holy Spirit drives him out to the desert to be tempted by Satan in a confrontation of forty days, reminiscent of Moses in the wilderness of Sinai and the prophet Elijah on Mount Horeb. Typical of apocalyptic writing, these images connect the ministry of Jesus with the record of God's great deeds of salvation in the past. They move the desert scene out of the geographico-historical realm into that of theological symbolism. It was in the desert that Moses and Elijah were tested and where they encountered God's call to leadership for the salvation of God's people (Exod 3:1–8; 1 Kings 19:8–18). Jesus will present a new covenant on his return from the desert, a covenant that he will ratify with his blood.

At the end of his temptation or testing by the arch power of evil in the desert, Jesus' presence among wild beasts and protection by the angels continue the apocalyptic imagery of his call by God. They show that he will emerge victorious over the supernatural powers of evil throughout his ministry and death on the cross. Thus Mark begins his story of the arrival of the Kingdom in which the reality of the terrestrial world is clarified by Jesus' actions on the supernatural level of salvation history. Here and in all the exorcism stories Jesus has ultimate power from God over the kingdom of Satan, the celestial symbol of the oppressive reign of Rome and of the oppression of its aristocratic client-rulers in Palestine. The first-century reader understands that Mark is showing that the ultimate victory over the anti-God forces of evil has been won by Jesus, as Mark employs the traditions about Jesus' exorcisms to inform the readers/auditors just how complete that victory was.

The Evangelist reinforces the traditions of Jesus' success over the demons by his summary statements about Jesus' fame as an exorcist (1:28, 34, 39; 3:11) and shows that Jesus can delegate power over demons to his followers (3:14–15; 6:7, 13). In the first of Jesus' exorcisms (1:21–28), we see that a possessed man has been personally invaded by a powerful force that renders him "unclean," that is, unable to participate in his own community's social and religious life. The demon knowingly fears the eschatological power *(exousia)* of Jesus and tries to sidetrack him by the magical tactic of naming his true identity to gain power over him. The demon is right: Jesus truly is "the Holy One of God," the counterpart to all unholiness or uncleanness of the demonic world, because his power/authority *(exousia)* is from God, the center of all holiness.[1] Jesus silences the demon effortlessly and frees the man of the demon, which departs from him with a violent but impotent convulsion.

The Jerusalem scribes recognize the power of Jesus over the demons as greater than their own, so they must impute it to some more powerful personal being. As minions of the oppressive Temple regime they will not reckon it truly as power from God, whose power on earth they claim to mediate by their exploitative system of tithes, taxes, and sacrifice fees. They therefore ascribe it to possession by the devil "Beelzebul" (literally, "the lord of the household = this world"): "By the prince of demons he drives out demons" (3:22). Jesus fires back an irrefutable argument that it couldn't be Satan who was driving out his own minions and speaks a proverb that epitomizes his own eschatological ministry: "No one can enter a strong man's house to plunder his property unless he first ties up the strong man" (3:27). In this way Jesus clarifies his actions as plundering the "chattel" of the so-called lord of this world, that is, regaining for God the freedom of God's children who have been enslaved by evil power.

The story of the Gerasene Demoniac is highly symbolic for Mark (5:1–20). Jesus again confronts an unclean spirit but this time demands control over the demon by forcing it to reveal its true name. When the demon answers, "Legion is my name," Mark identifies for us the source of the greatest evil in the land, the occupation forces of the Roman Empire, which legitimate the exploitative Temple religion and use it for their own profit. The "Legion" try to trick him by pleading for clemency, but Jesus outwits them and sends them, filthy swine that they are, to their destruction in the chaos of the sea, to perish just as the soldiers of Pharaoh did in the first Exodus.[2]

In the narrative of the Syrophoenician Woman (7:24–30), Jesus' liberating power over demons is shown to be effective even for those outside of Israel. Mark's Jesus is not above learning from the grace of God embodied even in a faith-filled outsider. If he had not considered up until now the entry into the Kingdom of those who do not belong to God's Chosen People, he is made aware of it by this courageous woman's faith and her love for her daughter.

In the account of the Epileptic Boy, Mark makes the point of how the followers of Jesus are to continue his ministry of freeing enslaved people from their demons. When asked to show compassion, Jesus responds that "everything is possible to one who has faith" (9:23). The boy's father has only weak faith, but that does not stop Jesus from completely ridding the boy of the demon. Why, then, could the disciples not drive it out? they ask him in private. Jesus' answer is very instructive for Mark's community, since they are to cast out demons in their ministry of preaching the gospel, just as Jesus did. "He said to them, 'This kind can only come out through prayer'" (9:29). Since Jesus has not said a prayer in this exorcism, he must mean that power over evil comes from a prayerful life, and not from possession of some magical power. Power for Christians is always power from God, and never a manipulation of the divine. Mark confirms this point at the end of the episode, where Jesus teaches that the task of the church is not to control his power/authority over evil, but to *welcome* anyone found "driving out demons in your name" (9:38), for that is a sign of their prayerful faith in him and in the power of God. No one who is effective in performing miracles in Jesus' name can ever be against the memory of Jesus or against what God wills for the Christian community. Even if someone only gives a believer a cup of water, they will be rewarded (9:41).

THE PARABLE CHAPTER (CHAPTER 4)

Jesus has shown in his teaching that every moment of the present is an eschatological *kairos* since the Kingdom of God is "at hand" (1:15), present in potential for any who would enter it by doing God's will. As Mark emphasizes over and over again, the opportunity for repentance and entrance into the Kingdom is the preaching of the "word," which is the gospel (see 1:38; 3:14; 13:10; 14:9). The Mystery of the Kingdom (4:11) is the act of entering it, that is, of actually living God's will. This is the key to understanding the Kingdom: one must know it from the inside by participating in it. "Mystery," in Daniel 12 and in contemporaneous Jewish writings, refers to the secret plan of God to bring "this age" to a close and to inaugurate the new eschatological era. Mark uses the collection of parables here in chapter 4 to show that the Kingdom is God's eschatological plan to bring about the next stage of salvation for the world in those who follow Jesus in doing God's will.

The whole parable chapter is apocalyptic, suggesting the eschatological battle between God and Satan over the produce of the "seed," as predicted in the parable about the Binding of the Strong Man (Satan).[3] The parable of the Seed Sown (4:3–8) and its explanation (4:14–20) show just how this struggle takes place. The preaching of the word sows the seed of a new life in the Kingdom, but a variety of responses to this calling by God are possible. The seed sown on the path is really a metaphor for all who hear the word and refuse to accept it. The power of evil, personified by Satan, is strong against the reform of an unjust world by those who would do God's will. Satan swoops in immediately like some predatory bird to eliminate growth from the very beginning of the conversion process.

In the next two images we see how Satan works to undermine the repentance and commitment to new life of those who might be receptive to God's word. The rocky ground is the image for suffering in the Christian life, for as Jesus foretells, every Christian must take up the cross and die him- or herself to follow him. Jesus will elaborate on this theme in his other great discourse in Mark, the Eschatological Discourse of chapter 13, where he discloses the necessity of tribulation in the Christian life. The third metaphor, that of the thorns, at first does not seem to match its meaning of "worldly anxiety, the lure of riches, and the craving for other things," (v. 19) for these enticements appear to be very attractive to us. However, the result of their ugly work is quite like the effect of a thorny overgrowth on a newly planted field. Thorns choke the life out of the crop by taking away both its water and its sunlight, leaving it without nourishment and with little possibility for growth. At the opposite end of the spectrum is the rich growth of the seed that falls on rich soil. Those "who hear the word and accept it and bear fruit" (v. 20) can yield a fantastic crop of twice, four times, and even seven times the usual fourteenfold produce of agriculture.

The parable of the Seed Growing (4:26–29) is also an eschatological metaphor for the success of the Kingdom. God initiates the action of the Kingdom without human help and brings about its growth in ways completely mysterious to the world. Here again we are presented with the heavenly reality behind the apparent failure of Jesus and his Kingdom on earth. Only God knows this reality fully and will reap the eschatological harvest when God will decide that "the grain is ripe" (v. 29), for as we learn later, "of that day or hour no one knows . . . but only the Father" (13:32).

Before he returns to Jesus' healing ministry, Mark closes the Parable Chapter with an apocalyptic incident on the Sea of Galilee. This is the first of two crossings in which Mark, calling to mind the primordial myth of the warrior king battling the sea, symbolizes Jesus' hidden power/authority *(exousia)* over nature and the demonic elements that lurk behind its violence (4:35–41; 6:45–52). In ancient Near Eastern mythology, the prime symbol of chaos is the sea. Jesus "rebukes" the wind and silences the sea with just the same language and actions he uses to cast out demons (Jesus "rebukes" demons in 1:25; 3:12; 9:25). His easy dominance over the dangerous forces of nature as well as over the demonic world show that in the supernatural realm, God's realm, Jesus has complete power to save from the forces of evil all who would follow him into the Kingdom of God.

ESCHATOLOGY IN PART 2 OF THE GOSPEL

Apart from the evenly spaced exorcisms in chapters 5, 7, and 9, it is not until later in part 2 of the Gospel that we encounter another explicitly eschatological text. This was to be expected, since in part 1 of the Gospel Mark deals mainly with the identity of Jesus and the arrival of the Kingdom in his ministry. In part 2, however, because of the reactions of the religious leaders and the response of his own disciples to his teaching, Jesus comes to two conclusions. First, he now fully understands that the religious leaders see him and his idea of the Kingdom of God as a threat to their dominance of the Jewish people and to the extraordinary prosperity that they enjoy because of it. Jesus perceives that, as Mark's narrative has repeatedly shown, they are out to destroy him and his dangerous message.

Second, Jesus turns to the preparation of his disciples for when he must leave them until he will return in glory. Mark has pointedly demonstrated in the narrative that the disciples frequently do not understand (4:10, 38; 5:31; 6:37, 49–52; 7:17–18; 8:4), and even misunderstand (1:37–38; 8:16–21) Jesus' words and actions. Jesus knows from this that they have followed him mostly with the hope of their own aggrandizement in some new politico-religious regime with him as leader, the powerful and lordly Messiah of popular expectation.[4] It is here in part 2 of Mark's narrative that Jesus has to face their mistaken understanding head-on and to speak freely of the difficulties in their future if they should carry on his work in the Kingdom of God.[5] Jesus knows that his fate at the hands of the powerful Temple religion has been sealed. He states it clearly in 8:31, that he "must suffer greatly and be rejected by the elders, the chief priests, and the scribes, and be killed," the aristocratic ruling class and their minions. Mark underscores this reality by Jesus' repetition of this prediction of his Passion in 9:31 and 10:33–34, and, of course, in the narration of his symbolic action at the Last Supper, when he gives over his body and blood "which will be shed for many" (14:24). This reality has serious consequences for the disciples, who must now understand the full requirements of their entry into the Kingdom of God.

Jesus begins his new teaching by asking them their true thoughts about his identity: "But who do you say that I am?" (8:29). Peter's reply, "You are the Messiah," confirms their mistaken identification of him as the *lordly* messiah and explains all their previous misunderstanding of his ministry. He quickly silences them and radically corrects their idea by "teaching" them *(didaskein)* that he, as the Son of Man, must suffer and die before his resurrection after three days (8:31). Yes, he is the Son of Man, the Human One that Daniel predicted would come to God's glorious presence to bring a truly human rule to all the world, "an everlasting dominion / that shall not be taken away, / [whose] kingship shall not be destroyed" (Dan 7:14). But this can happen only after the beastly rulers of Daniel's chapter 7 will have "lost their dominion" (Dan 7:12). They, now in the form of the elders, the chief priests, and the scribes, will lose their dominion precisely in the act, Jesus foretells, of attempting to destroy all that God wants for him and for all human beings. When they think that they have extinguished life, freedom, and justice (the Kingdom) by their execution of Jesus, God will counter their injustice by raising Jesus up to new life after three days. God alone has the ultimate power over life and death!

Peter's altercation with Jesus that follows shows that Jesus was right: Peter actually *rebukes* Jesus for predicting that he must suffer and die. The disciples never imagined their role in Jesus' mission when he chose them to "be with him" (3:14) and when he sent them out to preach repentance and the new attitude of sharing that the Kingdom of God demands (6:7–13). Instead, they still share in their own way the self-interest of the ruling elite, since they would like to replace them in glory and power. Mark documents this appraisal of the disciples amply in the stories that follow. At the Transfiguration, Peter's mistake was to try to bask in Jesus' glory by setting up three tents in which they could remain far from the needs of God's people and their task of preaching the gospel (9:5).[6] Further, the questions of the disciples about which of them was the greatest (9:33–34) and about a place in glory with Jesus (10:35–37) confirm their self-centeredness and the refusal of their commission, even *after* Jesus has clarified his teaching here in 8:34–38.

To clarify the real demands of discipleship, Mark has Jesus summon the crowd (and all of us who would listen to his words) to join his disciples for a new teaching on the requirements of the Kingdom. He asks them to renounce themselves and to join him in living only for God, knowing that life, the power to be fully human, is offered unconditionally and without defense by God to human freedom. He now knows that to do this a disciple must be willing to share in his fate, "to . . . deny [oneself], take up [one's] cross, and follow me" (8:34).

In the following verses Jesus highlights the two ways (8:33) of thinking about salvation.[7] "Human thinking" means to preserve this life at all cost, believing that death is the annihilation of all that one is. Conversely, "thinking as God does" is to trust in God and make Jesus' ideal one's own, to believe that death does not signify the end, but that it can be the crowning event of human development. To choose the first is to choose a life of slavery, because then those who can harm physical health will always have controlling power over one. To choose to live for others, conversely, frees one from selfish concern about death to dedicate oneself to the good of human life, that is, to God's will.

Jesus explains in verses 35–37 that in the present *kairos,* the only way to save one's life is to risk it for Jesus and for the sake of the Kingdom that the gospel proclaims. "Life" here (*psychē* in Greek) means much more than merely being alive before one's death. For that Mark has another word (*bios).* In Greek, *psychē* means "life" as the center of a person's human activities, of feeling and emotions, desire and enjoyment. Jesus teaches that to seek earthly power will in fact ruin that life by ending the growth in faith and love that God has planned for each person.

In verse 38 Jesus warns the disciples (and us) that not choosing to follow him now, by refusing to live a life of unselfish and universal love for others, not to risk public identification with the cause of Jesus, will bring about dire consequences of one's own making. Those who refuse to collaborate with God's plan for the betterment of all will not be recognizable to the Son of Man when he comes to gather his elect. For they will have curtailed their human development and frustrated their potential for the fullness of human being, the very characteristics that the Son of Man will look for when he comes.

After Jesus shares a glimpse of his coming glory with his intimate circle of disciples, Peter, James, and John, in the Transfiguration, and predicts his death and resurrection again (9:31), he goes on to declare what true greatness in the Kingdom requires. One must be as powerless as a child and the servant of all who come in Jesus' name (9:35–37). In 9:42–48 he states clearly the harsh negative results of sin for all who would be saved, "to go/be thrown into Gehenna," mentioned three times in opposition to the desired entrance into life/the Kingdom.

Jesus' words "to enter into the Kingdom" and its parallel phrase, "to enter into life," refer to the present life of the disciple who does God's will. He then explains that Gehenna, the biblical symbol for eschatological judgment and punishment, is the reward for sinners. He says that it is a place "where 'their worm does not die, and the fire is not quenched'" (9:48), citing Isa 66:24, where the corpses of those who rebel against God are to be piled outside Jerusalem. That same text of Isaiah predicts that a new heaven and a new earth will appear (Isa 66:22) when God comes to gather the nations to see God's glory (Isa 66:18). Thus here Jesus underscores his teaching of 8:35–38 by reminding us all of the eschatological vision of the Book of Isaiah, in order that the energy from the past revelation to Israel awaken firm resolve within those Jesus wants to form for the Kingdom in the present.[8] He concludes that it is better for his followers radically to cut out the causes of scandal for the "little ones" (v. 42) now than to be "thrown into Gehenna" and abandoned by God at the Eschaton.

In the next chapter Mark narrates the encounter (discussed above in chap. 3) by Jesus of the Rich Man, who asks what he must do to inherit "eternal life" (10:17). The phrase "eternal life" appears twice in this section and only a few times elsewhere in the Synoptic Gospels. Since the phrase is introduced by an obviously Jewish man, we can presume that the fellow is asking about life after death and resurrection, since that is its meaning in other Jewish literature of this period.[9] Jesus begins his answer with the mandate to keep the Ten Commandments, the typical requirement in the Old Testament for "life," that is, the ability to live vitally and morally in this world. The man departs in denial of Jesus' challenge to him to give all he has to the poor so that he will "have treasure in heaven." In the ensuing discussion, Jesus points out that God's salvation is an ongoing process that begins with entrance to the Kingdom, an action that requires repentance and belief in the gospel, as Jesus has proclaimed (1:15). This acknowledgment of the presence of God in a person's life enables one to do God's will, to give up reliance on personal wealth and power, and thus "to enter the Kingdom of God." Such repentance is the way one starts on the way to eternal salvation or "eternal life," something that a (dishonestly) rich person cannot do. When Peter asks what their reward will be for giving up everything to follow him, Jesus tells of the concrete rewards of the Kingdom by promising a hundredfold "in this present age . . . and eternal life in the age to come." Thus Jesus corrects and amplifies the common Jewish notion of "eternal life" by showing that salvation is not a completely future reality.

We may conclude that in this section the phrases "eternal life," "treasure in heaven," to "be saved," and "eternal life in the age to come" all refer to the typical first-century understanding of the eschatological future God has in store for the world and for each individual found worthy of it. Jesus maintains, however, that this goal may be achieved only by entrance into the Kingdom of God in *this* life by doing God's will *now*, a course of action the Rich Man would not follow. Thus, he says, "many that are first" *now* among the rich and powerful in this world "will be last" in regard to a place in the Kingdom of God (10:31). Their future is up to the mercy of God, fortunately, and "all things are possible for God" (10:27).

After Jesus has predicted his death and resurrection for a third time (10:33–34), the disciples James and John ask him to have positions of honor "in your glory" (10:37). In his answer Jesus affirms that God has prepared just such an eschatological scenario, although it "is not mine to give but is for those for whom it has been prepared" (10:40). Jesus, who has already predicted his resurrection and his return as the Son of Man in glory, takes this opportunity to reaffirm his teaching on the affliction they must first endure. The glory "has been prepared" only for those who can "drink the cup that I drink [and] be baptized with the baptism with which I am baptized" (10:38).

ESCHATOLOGY IN PART 3 OF THE GOSPEL

In Mark 12 Jesus takes on each group of the religious leadership in Jerusalem and defeats them soundly. Of interest to us here is the altercation initiated by the Sadducees on the question of the afterlife (12:23–27). Not much is known about this group of ruling elites, other than their acceptance of only the first five books of the Bible, the Pentateuch, as Sacred Scripture, plus their vehement rejection of the resurrection, attested in the New Testament, the ancient historian Flavius Josephus, and in rabbinic documents.[10]

They pose a conundrum to Jesus that they think will reduce to absurdity the common Jewish belief in resurrection on the last day. They choose a passage from the heart of the Pentateuch, the "Levirate Law" (Deut 25:5–10), and pose a dilemma about the childless woman of their question. It is obvious that they can only consider any life after the resurrection to be a mere continuance of this life, the life where they have all the power and control. Jesus attacks the very heart of their conceit when he quotes perhaps the most famous Pentateuchal saying of and about God from Exod 3:6, "I am . . . the God of Abraham, the God of Isaac, the God of Jacob." Jesus' harsh retort is that they know neither the Scripture nor the power of God (12:24). Their main interest in Scripture is how to protect their social advantage, in this case the political and economic stability of the patriarchal family system that keeps them in power. They don't see the true meaning of Scripture in Exod 3:6, namely that the patriarchs are alive in God's keeping.

Jesus' second point is that they do not understand God's lordly power over life and death if they do not believe that God can raise people from the dead. What is important here for our study of Marcan eschatology is that Jesus argues that the resurrection clearly exists for all and that resurrection life belongs to the divine realm, a different state of being, something "like the angels in heaven," who are constantly with God (12:25).

The next text in the Gospel that we must study in our search for Mark's eschatological teaching is the great Eschatological Discourse of chapter 13. We shall have a full discussion of it in our final chapter, but let us first look at a few other texts at the end of the Gospel.

Jesus predicts "I shall not drink again the fruit of the vine until the day when I drink it new in the kingdom of God" (14:25). This language alludes to the expectation of the "messianic banquet," a feature common enough in first-century Jewish literature, which promises that the glorious coming of the messiah will be accompanied by the sharing of the abundant food and drink of the messianic age.[11] Jesus, of course, knows this tradition and uses it to affirm his unswerving belief in the joyful times to come in the Kingdom. He assures that it will be he whom the messianic banquet (the eucharist?) will celebrate when he returns after his upcoming death and resurrection.

"That day" is a common way of referring to the fulfillment by God of Israel's eschatological hopes, as in Zech 14:9: "The LORD shall become king over the whole earth . . . *on that day.*" This is exactly the ultimate triumph that Jesus has assured his disciples about the Kingdom/Kingship of God.

In 14:28 Jesus says, "but after I have been raised up, I shall go before you to [in] Galilee," and the mysterious young man announces to the women at Jesus' empty tomb in 16:7 that "he is going before you to [in] Galilee; there you will see him, as he told you." As we have seen above, this image refers to the disciples' own "Galilee," their journey in preaching the Gospel and enduring the suffering and rejection it brings about. But Jesus promises "to go before" them after he has been crucified, to lead them as a shepherd does his flock, so that their lives of faith in God and sharing with God's people will have clear direction.

In the "place named Gethsemane," (14:32) where Jesus prays in his trouble and distress at his upcoming death, he finds that his inner circle of disciples—Peter, James and John—have fallen asleep instead of keeping watch (14:32–37). He says to Peter, their leader, "Watch and pray that you may not undergo the test" (14:38). The Greek word *peirasmos* can mean "test, trial, or temptation," and scholars have interpreted it in this passage in many ways. Although it is used only here in Mark's Gospel, it probably shares some of the eschatological meaning of the petition at the end of the Lord's Prayer in Matthew and Luke, "and do not subject us to the final test" (Matt 6:13; Luke 11:4). In Mark, the verb form of the word, *peirazō* ("to tempt, try, or test"), occurs four times, once when Jesus is tempted in the desert by Satan (1:13) and three times when he is tested in his preaching by the Pharisees (8:11; 10:2; and 12:15 joined with the Herodians). There is no equivocation here, because in Mark's symbolic universe the religious and political leadership (that of the Pharisees and Herodians) is merely a tool of Satan's power. I think that Jesus is saying to Peter (and the others), "You'd better pray that you are not tested by Satan or by any of those who do his dirty work, because you are definitely not ready for it!" In response they did not, in fact, pray, but fell asleep again, and when the test came with the crowd waving their swords and clubs to arrest Jesus, they all ran away. Peter became the classic failure when he later denied three times that he even knew Jesus.

The final text we must discuss is Jesus' answer to the high priest's question, "Are you the Messiah, the son of the Blessed One?" Jesus says, "I am; and 'you will see the Son of Man seated at the right hand of the Power and coming with the clouds of heaven'" (14:61–62). But that he is the glorious Son of Man who will be seen coming of the clouds is almost exactly what Jesus has said at the climax of the Eschatological Discourse. We shall examine that text now in order to make a finally summary and conclusion on Jesus' eschatological message in the Gospel of Mark.

NOTES

1. See Joel Marcus's helpful explanation of the eschatological quality of both Jesus' "power" (*exousia*, as parallel to "kingdom" *[basileia]* in Dan 7:14, 27; Rev 12:10; 17:12) and his being "holy," in his Anchor Bible Commentary *Mark 1–8* (New York: Doubleday, 2000), 191–93.

2. The symbolic interpretation of this scene is very natural for a Latin American scholar such as João Wenzel; see his *Pedagogia de Jesus segundo Marcos* (São Paulo: Ed. Paulinas, 1997), 71–72.

3. Sharyn Dowd makes this insightful point in *Reading Mark: A Literary and Theological Commentary on the Second Gospel* (Reading the New Testament; Macon, Ga.: Smyth & Helwys, 2000), 49.

4. José Maria González Ruiz comes to this sad but all-too-true conclusion in *Evangelio según Marcos: Introducción, traducción, comentario* (Estella: Verbo Divino, 1988), 145.

5. Once again, I am deeply indebted to Carlos Bravo in the following section on Mark 8:29–38 (*Jesús, hombre en conflicto,* 155–57).

6. João Luiz Correia Júnior, "A pedagogía da missão," *EstBib* 64 (1999): 68.

7. Juan Mateos and Fernando Camacho, *Marcos: Texto y Comentario* (Córdoba, Spain: El Almendro, 1994), 169.

8. Carlos Mesters, *The Hope of the People Who Struggle: The Key to Reading the Apocalypse of St. John* (Athlone, South Africa: Theology Exchange Program, 1994), 21.

9. Apart from the parallels to this section of Mark, the phrase occurs in Matt 25:46; Mark 10:30; Luke 10:25, and it refers to resurrected life after death in the Septuagint in Dan 12:2; 4 Macc 15:3; cf. 2 Macc 7:9, and at Qumran in 1QS 4:7.

10. For a full discussion of the Sadducees see Anthony J. Saldarini, *Pharisees, Scribes, and Sadducees in Palestinian Society* (Grand Rapids, Mich.: Eerdmans, 1988), chaps. 5 and 13.

11. For example, in the Dead Sea Scrolls, "And then the Messiah of Israel shall come . . . and they shall gather for the common table to eat and to drink *new wine*" (1QSa 2:14–17); "On this mountain [*"on that day,"* v. 9] the LORD of hosts / will provide for all the peoples / A feast of rich food and choice wines" (Isa 25:6).

—6—

THE MARCAN ESCHATOLOGICAL
DISCOURSE (CHAPTER 13)

Before we tackle the great Eschatological Discourse of Jesus, it will be good to remind ourselves of the big picture presented up to this point in the Gospel by Mark. The narrative has been describing the "good news" of God's salvation that began in Jesus of Nazareth, the gospel both preached by Jesus and the gospel about Jesus, the Messiah/Son of God who teaches about the Kingdom of God. This Kingdom is a human community where all are welcome and where injustice has no place. It has been inaugurated by Jesus' life-for-others, the Teacher who predicts that it will come in power when he rises after his death-for-others. In the first part of the narrative Jesus is presented as a powerful teacher by whose authority/power *(exousia)* the Kingdom of God has already arrived in his teaching and his miraculous restoration of the marginalized to their proper place in society. In the Gospel's middle section (8:27–10:52) Jesus tries to teach his followers how the Kingdom will come in power in himself in his upcoming death. The Kingdom can manifest itself in them, too, but only if they follow his lead by doing what God wants, a course of action that will bring them suffering and affliction as well.

In the final part of the Gospel (11:1–16:8), Jesus lives out his teaching by confronting the oppressive religious system symbolized by the Temple, and then being given over to its minions to the death he foreknew. Before his untimely death, however, he is able to give his disciples instructions in a great Eschatological Discourse on how to live in the difficult times ahead. After his tragic death in chapter 15, a mysterious young man (the Evangelist himself?) announces to some women disciples that Jesus has been raised from the dead and "that he is going before you in Galilee." This means that the Risen Jesus will lead the way to God in the Kingdom if only they retrace the steps of his life-for-others starting in their own Galilee, and dedicate their lives to the preaching and witness of the gospel.

THE CONTEXT OF THE DISCOURSE

The eschatological discourse of Mark 13 comes at the end of a literary unity in chapters 11–12, in which Jesus breaks with every oppressive power of official religion. He subverts the desire for the traditional Davidic Messiah by his prophetic entrance to Jerusalem on a lowly donkey (11:1–11), and by his question about Psalm 110 (12:35–37). He denies the legitimacy of the Temple by his actions and reactions to the commerce in it (11:15–19 and 12:41–44) and enters into confrontation with the Sanhedrin (the chief priests, scribes, and elders), the Pharisees, Herodians, and the Sadducees in a definitive rupture with no turning back. After he handles the traps of all these power groups, Jesus takes his most intimate disciples aside in chapter 13. He instructs them on how to deal with the adversity to be caused by the hatred and misunderstanding of others when he would be absent in the future, at the destruction of the Temple and afterward in the face of new enemies of the gospel.

The connection to chapters 11–12 is very important because the whole section of chapters 11–13 forms a literary unit that focuses on the double theme of the downfall of the old Temple-centered religious domination and the birth of a new community of God that replaces the Temple. The new community will break all the bonds of religious exclusivism and oppression to become a new "house of prayer for all peoples" (11:17) as a result of Christian preaching "to all nations" (13:10). It will thus collaborate in God's saving work in the downfall of oppression and the forming of a new and just world community, the Kingdom of God.

THE GENRE OF MARK 13

The Eschatological Discourse (13:5–37) is a long exhortation of Jesus that shares some of the main characteristics of current Jewish apocalyptic literature. It emphasizes that all that is to come has been determined by God, and it predicts the arrival of a savior figure and the fate of the righteous, who must go through much affliction (the "eschatological woes"). It does not, however, illustrate any of the other usual elements, namely, apocalyptic judgment or the fate of the wicked, and is quite ambiguous about the arrival of the End. Rather than being a description of the world to come, as are most apocalypses, the entire Discourse is an exhortation dotted with imperatives that give direction to the disciples for living the *present* difficult life.[1]

Thus Mark presents us with a hybrid genre, an apocalyptic parenesis (exhortation) which, on the one hand, uses traditional apocalyptic imagery (esp. in the "woes" of vv. 7–8, 14–17, and most plainly in the vision of the Coming of the Son of Man in vv. 24–27), in which Jesus guarantees the final victory of the Kingdom of God. Mark uses the apocalyptic genre to present Jesus as the heavenly seer of the past (namely, of 30 C.E., the year in which he died). He predicts the events surrounding the Jewish war against the Romans and their destruction of the Temple (66–70 C.E.), events contemporaneous with the writing of the Gospel. Having established such credibility, he can go on to assure the salvific outcome of history, no matter how long it takes and how much suffering it might involve. On the other hand, the main feature of the Discourse is its many commands, and this establishes it as a complete parenesis, an exhortation which gives instructions for Christian discipleship throughout the full course of history.

The Discourse explains that the present difficulties in Mark's community were foreordained by God by the apocalyptic technique of rereading the Scriptures. The powerful words of the prophets Daniel, Isaiah, Jeremiah, Ezekiel, Zechariah, and Joel are revisited by Jesus, who applies their symbolic language to a new context. Jesus does not predict a future apocalyptic destruction of the world, but reveals the meaning of history as an urgent call for his followers to preach the gospel under the guidance of the Holy Spirit. He exhorts them to believe his words and have hope in the struggle for a new world when he, as the glorious Son of Man, will gather together all the world's people who come to believe (v. 27).

THE STRUCTURE OF MARK 13

Mark probably used some traditional material in composing this Eschatological Discourse, but it is notoriously difficult to identify the exact sources used in any particular text of Mark. When scholars try to isolate the early traditions Mark had at hand, they inevitably seem unable to agree among themselves and often contradict each other. Moreover, source critics have often misunderstood an important strategy Mark used because he was writing for a *listening* audience and not for the individual reader. When the text contains the repetition of a term or phrase in the same sentence or shortly thereafter, Mark is not fumbling with sources, but underlining what he wants to emphasize, and often how he wants to *redefine* an idea.[2] For example, the verb "to say" is used three times in verse 11 because what and how Christians are to speak when they are being persecuted is very important. Whole ideas are also repeated to make a point. Thus Jesus warns against imposters twice (vv. 5–6 and 21–23) because they are a very real threat to the community. He denies the predictability of "the Day" three times (vv. 32, 33, 35), addresses the destruction of the Jerusalem Temple three times (vv. 5–7, 14–19, 28–29), and alludes to the coming tribulation three times as well (vv. 7–9, 24–25, 30).

Thus, whatever sources he might have used, we can see that in the final form of the text, that is, the Gospel text as we have it now, Mark has constructed a flowing discourse, full of art and effect. Our description of its structure may appear to be somewhat complicated, but the outline in the chart below should make it clear that, after the introduction, Mark has composed a unified speech with an introduction and three related parts. In its (double) introduction, Jesus definitively breaks with the Jerusalem Temple by predicting its utter destruction (vv. 1–2). Then, the question of the Four shows that they miss the point by focusing on the unknowable times of future events (vv. 3–4), and sets up the lengthy response of Jesus (vv. 5–37).

The Discourse proper contains three sections, but they do not describe three different chronological periods. They give us three different pictures of the same realities, with new information added in each. The ancient audience would hear the reading of this part of the Gospel with much the same effect as we moderns get from the triple visual presentation of the same scene in a movie. For example, in the dress shop scene in Quentin Tarantino's *Jackie Brown,* the audience learns something more in each new view of the one interaction. John Collins identifies this kind of "redundance" in the Book of Daniel where the picture of the crisis at Antioch (in Daniel 7) is further described by three parallel revelations (chaps. 8, 9, 10–12) that repeat the same events in slightly different ways. He goes on to say that the technique "is crucially important," since "the apocalypses are not conveying a 'literal' or univocal truth that can be expressed in one exclusive way."[3] Seán Kealy shows how similar re-presentations of the same events occur in the Book of Revelation 6 (the seven seals), 8–9 (the seven trumpets), and 16 (the seven bowls). They each describe "the whole story of the Christian Church moving through persecution to judgment and final triumph."[4]

In Mark each of the three sections can be divided into two smaller parts. Each subsection *a* begins with a response to the first part of the disciples' question in the introduction to the Discourse (v. 4): "When will this [namely, the destruction of the Temple] happen"? Each section then goes on to reply (subsection *b*) to the second component of the disciples' question in verse 4, the fulfillment of "all these things." In it Jesus describes how life is to be in the future mission of his faithful followers and how *divine power will assist it* (the Holy Spirit in v. 11, the Son of Man in v. 26, the return of the "man traveling abroad" in v. 34). Each of the resultant six subsections (except the fourth, 2.b., a pure apocalypse) is introduced by an imperative and completed by a concluding dictum (given in the parentheses in the chart below), which gives hope in "my words," the words of the Son of Man (v. 31). We can now give an outline of chapter 13 with the imperatives that begin and the aphorisms that close each subsection:

> Double introduction—destruction of Temple and question "When?" (vv. 1–4)
>
> 1. a. Wars and Rumors of War (vv. 5–8: "See"—"These are the . . . labor pains")
>   b. Persecution of Believers (vv. 9–13: "Watch"—"But the one who perseveres")
> 2. a. Siege of Jerusalem (vv. 14–23: "[They] must flee"—"I have told . . . you beforehand")
>   b. Coming of the Son of Man (vv. 24–27: *omitted*—"He will send out . . . and gather")
> 3. a. The Riddle of the Fig Tree (vv. 28–32: "Learn"—"No one knows . . . but only the Father")
>   b. Watching for the *kairos* (vv. 33–37: "Be watchful"—"What I say to you, I say to all")

VERSE BY VERSE EXEGESIS OF MARK 13

The Double Introduction

Verse 1. The odd, but typical, Marcan introduction of a new section with "and" *(kai)* ties in the scene of the discourse to the confrontation between Jesus and the powers of the old religious system in chapters 11–12. This showdown was begun and concluded in the Temple precincts. Now Jesus departs from the Temple, never to return, a prophetic sign that completes his earlier prophetic act against the Temple in 11:15–17.

As we have seen, Jesus condemns the Temple in Mark specifically for its unjust economic practices. His actions in 11:15–17 were against the merchants and moneychangers, but they were aimed higher, at the Temple priesthood's oppressive taxation and pay-for-sacrifice systems. This is made clear in 12:38–40 where he denounces the scribes for devouring the houses of *widows,* and then, "seated" in condemning judgment, he observes the Temple treasury where the system robs a *widow* of her whole livelihood (12:41–44).

The disciples, as usual, do not understand Jesus' criticism of the Temple in his departure from it and in his saying about the widow. Instead, they marvel at the splendor of the Temple buildings in Marcan irony as Jesus marvels at the injustice done to the widow. How difficult it is to deny the legitimacy of an institution that is so great and beautiful to look at! In a further irony, one of his disciples calls Jesus "teacher" even though he doesn't understand Jesus' *teaching* on the Temple. It has lost its validity as a "house of prayer" because it values wealth above the welfare of God's people, extorting money from the little that the poor possessed for the "obligatory" worship of their God.

Verse 2. Jesus' answer to the disciple, "Do you see?" reminds us of the blind man theme that frames part 2 of the Gospel ("Do you see anything?" 8:23; "Master, I want to see," 10:51). There Jesus tries rather unsuccessfully to instruct the disciples on how to live in the Kingdom of God. Now Jesus in this final teaching will repeat four times the command to "Really see!" (vv. 5, 9, 23, 33).

Jesus acknowledges the grandeur of the Temple by admitting that the buildings are *enormous* buildings in response to the disciple's exclamation in verse 1. Indeed, there was no need for a house of prayer to God to be so grand. For Jesus it had become a House of Mammon, a place of exploitation of the poor. In God's plan the Temple was supposed to reveal the true God to all of humanity ("a house of prayer for all peoples"; 11:17), but it failed, and its grandeur tried to cover its failure. Jesus announces its destruction in prophetic fashion just as Micah predicted the demolition of the First Temple for its greedy injustice (Mic 3:9–12). Jesus has already called it a "den of thieves" in 11:17, citing the prophet Jeremiah (7:11–14). Here in 13:2 Jesus deauthorizes the Temple with all its pretensions of being the center of salvation and predicts its complete disappearance.

Verse 3. The actual setup of the discourse begins in verse 3, where Jesus leaves the Temple area and goes to the Mount of Olives. Many of Mark's readers would know that the Mount of Olives is a special place for the Old Testament prophet Ezekiel on which "the glory of the LORD . . . took a stand" *after it had left the Temple* (Ezek 10:23). In Zech 14:2–4 God "will gather all the nations against Jerusalem for battle . . . [and] shall rest upon the Mount of Olives, which is *opposite* Jerusalem." Jesus now sits over against the Temple after having announced its complete destruction just as he sat over against the treasury when he observed the exploitation of the widow (12:41). He assumes a magisterial position in the symbolically divine sphere of a mountain by his "sitting on the Mount of Olives."[5] This sets the scene of the Discourse within Mark's double view of the heavenly reality of Jesus reflected in the historical account of his public ministry, such as we have already seen in the Transfiguration scene (9:2–8).[6] Jesus has condemned the Temple *spiritually* for its exploitation of the poor just as the Mount of Olives confronts it *physically.*[7]

The question posed by the four disciples at this the end of Jesus' ministry takes place "privately," just as Jesus gives special instruction to his disciples "privately" five other times in the Gospel. What follows is a secret (apocalyptic) revelation to the Four, the very first disciples Jesus called to share his preaching ministry. They will soon have to carry on without his earthly presence, as do all his future followers who are addressed by Mark's Gospel .

Verse 4. Like the Pharisees who also wanted "a sign" (Mark 8:11–12), the disciples are still looking for the restoration of national glory. Their double question, "When will this happen, and . . . when [will] all these things . . . end?" echoes the question of Dan 12:6—"When then [will be] the end? [of the destructive war which was to be the prelude to the full restoration of the Temple in 165 B.C.E.] . . . at the end of days" (Dan 12:9–13; cf. 11:35, Greek version, hereafter LXX). Like Daniel they hope that the misfortune of the Temple will compel God to rescue it from the power of foreign domination (Dan 9:17–19) by the violent intervention of those who would "take strong action" (Dan 11:32). The disciples presuppose that the destruction of Jerusalem will not be total, but that Jesus as messiah-savior will stop it and put an end to Roman oppression. In this way they try to negate the force of Jesus' announcement of the total destruction of the Temple and the system it represents.

The repetition of "these things" in the verse is not redundant: the first "these things" refers to an immediate antecedent, the destruction of the Temple, while the second phrase, "*all* these things," is proleptic of all the events after 70 C.E. mentioned in the following discourse, verses 5–37. A similar use of "these things . . . all these things" occurs in verses 29–30 and embraces all the events mentioned up to that point, including the coming of the Son of Man in verse 26.

Part 1 of the Discourse

WARS AND RUMORS OF WAR (VV. 5–8)

Verse 5. The disciples have asked about the End of the World but Jesus begins his response with cautions about events that are happening in *this* (the reader's) world. The many catastrophes and charlatans of stressful times tempt one into easy derailment from faith in God alone. The selfish aspirations of imminent apocalyptic thinking expect that God will suddenly intervene and remove all fear and suffering from life. Jesus calls this deception. There will be many "signs," but they will not signal the End of the World.

Verse 6. First, there will be a crowd of false "messianic" messengers as we see predicted by the prophets (Jer 14:15; 23:25; Zech 13:2–3). They will identify themselves by saying "I am," the response Jesus will use to affirm his identity as the Messiah to the High Priest before the Sanhedrin (14:62), when he will show his connection to the divine sphere and God's self-identification as "I am" in Exod 3:14. The impostors will affirm the false messianic hopes of restoration of the Davidic kingdom (as the disciples tried to in 10:37, 11:10, and 13:5), but, as Jesus points out in verses 7–8, God's will is the process of the liberation of the whole world.

Verse 7. Jesus goes on to point out that after the false messiahs and the Jewish War there will be even greater political unrest in the world and many future wars. These cataclysms, too, are necessary in the divine plan ("such things must happen").[8] Therefore, "do not be alarmed" at them. This verb is used in the entire New Testament in only two other texts: in the Matthean parallel to this text, "See that you are not alarmed" (Matt 24:6), and to warn against another false report "that the day of the Lord is at hand" (2 Thess 2:2). Wars are fatal. They are "not yet the end" that God has in mind. Why would one consider such negative violence to be God's crowning eschatological act? The "End" will not be the end of humanity; it will be the end of human oppression. It will be the end of that kind of world, but the commencement of the definitive and joyful community of humanity with God, where "there shall always be rejoicing and happiness / . . . / [and] the wolf and the lamb shall graze alike" (Isa 65:18, 25).

Verse 8. The plurality of nations and kingdoms at war refers to the future overthrow of the Roman and any other oppressive imperial powers that might hold back the fulfillment of God's plan, just as the repressive and exploitative Temple system did. By this prediction of further strife Mark's Jesus separates the Jewish War from the fulfillment of the messianic promise, thus fully dashing the disciples' hopes of a divine reversal of the inevitable destruction of the Jerusalem Temple. The "earthquakes" here are not to be understood literally, but are a common OT symbol of the violence of invasion (e.g., Isa 13:13; Jer 49:21; 51:29; Joel 2:10; Amos 8:8), and famine is the brutal result of war whenever it occurs. These wars are but the beginning of a long historical process, a time of stress and sorrow like a mother's "labor pains." But like the pain of childbirth, they are to bring about something good, a new life, a new world where the elect will be saved by the power and glory of the Son of Man (vv. 26–27).[9]

PERSECUTION OF BELIEVERS (VERSES 9–13)

Verse 9. The disciples are curious about the future of the Temple and the End of the World, but *now* is the time for them to "Watch out for yourselves." Corrupt society opposes the emancipation of people and the idea of a full human life for all, yet that is the true meaning of the gospel that Jesus' disciples will be commanded to preach in verse 10. The power structures of society will react violently to it. The persecution of innocent Christians is "as a witness before them [governors and kings]," a proof to God, and to all, of the oppressors' evil purpose. No one is fooled when the powerful abuse the freedom of those guilty of no crime but standing up for the truth.

Everyone can see how wrong such injustice was not only in the execution of Jesus and in the situation of the Christians of Mark's era who were involved in the Jewish War and Nero's persecution in Rome, but in the continuing abuse throughout history of true believers in Jesus. They have been "handed over" to the courts and synagogues (= today's local social and "religious" associations), and to governors and kings (= today's provincial and national government authorities) in too many contemporary countries as well. But theirs is the same fate as John the Baptist (1:14) and Jesus (9:31) who also were "handed over." The repetition of this verb later in verses 11 and 12 show how Mark focuses on the fate of Christians as similar to and because of their forebears in faith. They "will be hated by all because of my name," but they will receive salvation in the End (v. 13).

Verse 10. Before the End, before the Kingdom of God can arrive fully with Jesus as the Son of Man, the gospel must "first" be preached to all, just as the strong man must "first" (3:27) be tied up before his house (the domain of Satan) can be plundered. The necessity ("it is necessary") of this in God's plan is clear: if Christians fall back in their fears from their mission before the gospel is preached to all, the End process, the salvation of the world, comes to a stop and is just left hanging.[10]

Verse 11. But the disciple is not left alone in the mission. "Do not worry." One can have confidence that the same Holy Spirit that descended upon Jesus at the inception of his mission will be present. It will tell the disciple what to "say," in order that the proper witness (v. 9) that God wants for the Christian world mission be given. "In that hour," this assistance by the Spirit is nothing less than a personal communion of God with us, just as God inspired the prophets who suffered in denouncing the infidelity of the people, and Jesus who suffered in the "hour" of his death.[11] The price of announcing the gospel is high, but the declamation of the Holy Spirit through Jesus' disciples is absolutely necessary to convince the world of freedom and in freedom. Their refusal, however, to believe in the believers' witness to the gospel (v. 9) is blasphemy against the Holy Spirit, the only unforgivable sin (3:29), for it is the refusal of the salvation that Jesus offers.[12]

Verse 12. Oppressive powers have long known how to turn family members against one another. Siblings and children are rewarded for using their intimate information to betray the freedom of family members in many a totalitarian regime today. For Christians, a new family, a new "household" of the Lord ("a hundred times more"; 10:30; cf. 13:34) is begun in the unity of belief and suffering for the gospel of Jesus Christ.

Verse 13. The fear and the hatred by others that being misunderstood entails will bring the disciple to full maturity, to definitive salvation at the "end" of the disciple's life ("Whoever loses life for my sake and that of the gospel will save it"; 8:35), *and,* because of the resurrection, in the final salvific state of the world. Mark insists again and again in the pronouncements at the end of each subsection (vv. 8c, 13b, 23, 27, 31–32, 37) that God is in complete charge of history and that God's plan is fully known to Jesus. Thus all human life, and especially that of people of good faith who will have suffered and died throughout the history of the world, has meaning and will be vindicated at the End.

Constancy before God and solidarity with the mission of Christ is needed "up to the end" because "the End" is produced by it, by the preaching of the gospel. In the ancient present-oriented experience of time, the forthcoming future can be kept at a distance by those who refuse to spread God's will. We could even say with Juan Mateos that history is sped up or slowed down by the response of humans to the life-giving message of Jesus.[13] Indeed, although the End rests in the hands of God, God has tied it to the cooperation of believers since "the gospel *must* first be preached to all nations" (v. 10).

Part 2 of the Discourse

This second part of the Discourse is like a transparency that can overlay the first part, but which gives much more detail to the struggles leading up to the destruction of the Jerusalem Temple in its section *a* (vv. 14–23). Its section *b* (vv. 24–27), we believe, refers to the demise of the Temple and of all oppressive powers of a later time (those first mentioned in vv. 9–13) by the great power of the Son of Man who will come again and again in glory. As is typical in Jewish apocalyptic texts, the vision of the heavenly seer, here Jesus, includes predictions of what has already happened by the present time of the reader. As we explained above, using Carlos Mesters's analogy of the bus ride in Brazil, the accuracy of the description of past events assures the passengers/readers of the prediction of future events.

The Siege of Jerusalem (Verses 14–23)

Verse 14. "The desolating abomination," literally "the abomination of desolation," means something so horrible that it causes everyone to flee from it. It is the exact phrase used of the desecrating altar (or statue?) to Zeus Olympios set up in the Jerusalem Temple in 167–165 B.C.E. by Antiochus Epiphanes IV, and mentioned in 1 Mac 1:54; Dan 9:27; 11:31; 12:11. The general context of the Temple, however, is the only thing clear about Mark's use of it here. Two things show that the reference is cryptic. The parenthesis "let the reader understand" alerts us to its enigmatic character as a symbol, but Mark doesn't explain how the reader is to understand it. Second, while the Greek word for "abomination" *(bdelygma)* is of the neuter grammatical gender, the participle that modifies it is grammatically masculine, "[*him*] standing where he should not." Evidently the allusion is to some person.

This ambiguity does not surprise us, for another factor in nonliteral thinking is what John Collins has called "the essential multivalence of apocalyptic symbolism."[14] By this he means that although its literal reference is clear (here to the despicable act of Antiochus), an apocalyptic symbol may conjure up any number of historical or social realities in the thoughts of reader/listener. Scholars hotly dispute just what historical event this symbolic allusion from Mark's tradition refers to. It could remind the reader of any of a number of events in the first century, like the horror caused by a statue of Caligula proposed for erection in the Jerusalem Temple in 40 C.E. Other proposals are the arrival of the Roman army in Palestine in 66 C.E., the occupation of the Temple by Zealot leader Eleazar son of Simon in the winter of 67–68 C.E., the "false messiahs" Menahem Ben Judah or Simon Ben Giora later in Jerusalem, the (recent or forthcoming?) desecration of the Temple at the end of the Jewish War in 70 C.E., or some other foreseen repugnant event or person, like the "lawless one" mentioned in 2 Thess 2:3.

Perhaps Mark is being ambivalent here on purpose, including all the terrible tragedies that befell God's great Temple before its destruction. However, if forced to choose one opinion, the arrival of the Roman army in Palestine at the beginning of the Jewish War (ca. 66–67) seems to fit the scenario of Mark 13:14–18 best.[15] In it the "abomination" would refer to the human figure of the Roman general Vespasian, and "standing where he should not" would mean the establishment of the invading army by that commander who would soon be deified as Roman emperor. It would have been obvious that his intention was to march on the capital city of Jerusalem, and so flight to the safety of the hill country would be good advice indeed. The absolute identification of the "abomination of desolation" is perhaps impossible for us today, but it is not absolutely necessary for our understanding of Marcan eschatology.

"Standing where he *should* not": This phrase uses the same verb "it is necessary" *(dei)* we saw above in verse 7, but now in the negative. Since what "is necessary" is God's will, what is *not* "necessary" goes against it. Thus the abomination will not be from God, but will be a human calamity of revolution by a people who could tolerate oppression no more. Far from the will of God, the carnage of the Jewish War was the historical consequence of the injustice of the corrupt collaboration of the Jerusalem Temple aristocracy with the oppression of the Roman occupation.

Mark makes it clear, however, that the Danielic optimism about the Jerusalem Temple must not be falsely inferred here. In the Book of Daniel ("keep secret the message . . . until the end time"; 12:4), victory is assured within a set time known to God, when the Temple sacrifice is to be restored and when the archangel Michael will destroy the wicked (12:1–11). Here in Mark, however, such victory is precluded, for there is no indication for the termination of the "abomination" as in Dan 12:11. Moreover, Jesus has predicted the Temple's *total* destruction in verse 2. He had already shown the Jerusalem Temple to be like a fig tree full of leaves but not bearing fruit. Just as his curse caused the fig tree to wither up, so the Temple will be obliterated since it does not and cannot ever again give life (Mark 11:13–14, 20). To find true life the disciples of Jesus must abandon it and its defenders and so not be misled (13:22).

The flight and tribulation in this and the following five verses show that, while the destruction of Jerusalem will be complete, "the elect" will be saved, evidently to live on in history. "*Flee* to the *mountains*"—flight is the only recourse in the Bible to escape the destruction of a corrupt city, for example, at Sodom: "*flee* for your life! Get off to the *hills*" (Gen 19:17). The imperative, "flee," here also brings to mind a similar text from Jeremiah in which another evil city becomes the object of God's wrath: "Flee out of Babylon; / let each one save his life, / perish not for her guilt; / This is a time of vengeance for the LORD, / he pays her her due" (Jer 51:6; cf. 51:45; Isa 48:20). Thus the imperative of Jesus to flee from Judea also has a symbolic value. It means: "Abandon everything that the evil capital city stands for: oppression, love of power and the profound deceit of the religious system of the Temple. God will not preserve such a corrupt religious institution." The whole complex is about to collapse in face of the power of God who splits the Temple veil at the death of Jesus in 15:38.[16]

Verses 15–16. In a Discourse marked by a plethora of ideas in an economy of words, Mark elaborates the terrible danger of not responding immediately to the political situation when religious fanaticism enters the scene, as it did in the Jewish Revolt against Roman domination in the years 66 to 70 C.E., the time of the composition of this Gospel. Both those who are resting in the breeze on the rooftop, as well as people in the middle of their farming workday, must not linger but escape quickly whenever people try to use earthly force to bring about God's plan. All the religious factions who stayed in Jerusalem, who fought to defend their perception of God's will, were crushed by the imperial army. The only real power that exists to bring about a betterment of this world is total confidence in the power of God, a confidence that Jesus will soon demonstrate on the cross.

Verses 17–18. Jesus here shows God's compassion for the most vulnerable members of society, epitomized in its pregnant and nursing mothers. It seems that in prideful rebellions it is always the weak who suffer. Winter rains flood the usually dry *wadis* (creek beds) in Palestine and so Jesus advocates prayer that conditions not make the necessary escape all the more difficult. As in Jesus' life, so in the afflictions of his followers, prayer to a merciful God must be the constant companion.

Verse 19. "For those times will have tribulation such as has not been since the beginning of God's creation until now, nor ever will be." This verse clearly alludes to a text in the Book of Daniel about the occupation of the Temple by Antiochus: "that day of tribulation such as has not been since [nations] began until that time" (Dan 12:1, LXX). Mark's Jesus is now moving on in this verse from the beginning of the Jewish War to point out the virulence of the later events leading up to the destruction of the Temple itself in 70 C.E. He makes two changes to the text of Daniel. First, the tribulation in Palestine at that time will be greater than anything "from the beginning of creation" (not just "since nations began"); that is, the saying is extended to include all past human history, everything in the Bible, from Genesis on.

Second, as in the text of Daniel, Mark's Jesus points out that there had not been such tribulation up until that time, but then he adds, *"nor will there ever be"* anything like it again. By this radicalization of a text of Daniel, Jesus signals that the events of 70 C.E. are a dividing point in human history. All hope is now lost in the Temple and its religious system, which is about to be destroyed without any hope of being spared. God's plan for salvation must be carried out by others now, as Jesus has predicted in the parable of the Tenants after the master of the vineyard's son has been murdered, "He [the master] will come, put the tenants to death, and give the vineyard to *others*" (Mark 12:9). Those "others" are the Christians who will form the new household of prayer and preach the gospel to all nations.

Verse 20. God will lessen the distress of the purification of the "elect whom [God] chose," literally, "the elect whom God elected." This verse is often considered to be a pre-Marcan Jewish apocalyptic consolation because of the "Semitic redundancies" in the double use of "elect" and its repetition of the words "shortened the days." But we should not underestimate Mark's intention to emphasize by repetition. Jesus is predicting that Christians in war-torn Palestine should not despair. God has truly "shortened the days" of their (and that of all the elect's) tribulation so that they can and will "be saved."

"The elect whom God has elected" are no longer those who belong by birthright to the Temple religion. They are those who believe in Jesus and "witness" and "preach to all nations" (vv. 9, 10). They are the "elect" whom he will assure cannot be misled (v. 22), if only they are "watchful" (v. 23), and who will be "gathered" from their preaching mission to the ends of earth and sky (v. 27). Jesus has couched this assurance for the elect in the past tense ("[the Lord] did shorten the days"), since God has already planned mercy in this and every testing of the people of God. Here, we may point out, we have a good example of the apocalyptic assurance of the apparently *nonforthcoming* future by the heavenly seer we spoke about above. Jesus guarantees it as forthcoming because it already "is" in God's plan.

Verses 21–22. False messiahs and false prophets will perform signs and wonders, but Jesus the true Messiah performed no sign (8:12). In an overlay of verse 6 ("Many will come in my name"), Mark here alludes to the temptation to follow false spokespersons for God. They will appear on the scene with great pomp and conviction, a constant problem in past Jewish history (e.g., Deut 13:2–4), but especially in Jerusalem at the time of the destruction of the Temple (and in times of crisis up to our own day).[17]

Verse 23. Mark's Jesus has "told it all [i.e., all the foregoing] to you beforehand" as a call to vigilance to his faithful followers. By this, and by the aphorisms that close each subsection of the Discourse (vv. 8, 13b, 23, 27, 31–32, 37), he wants to confirm in them an absolute confidence in God's control of history, no matter what future opposition to the gospel might come to pass.

THE COMING OF THE SON OF MAN (VERSES 24–27)

Verses 24–25. At this point in the Discourse a cosmic cataclysm is announced, a turning point "after that tribulation," (v. 24) that is, after the unparalleled tribulation of the siege of Jerusalem by the Roman army mentioned earlier (v. 19). The plainest sense of these verses is this: Jesus is saying here that after the arrival of the Roman army in Palestine in 66 C.E. (vv. 14–18), and after the siege of Jerusalem in 69–70 C.E. with its false prophets and messiahs (vv. 19–22), the disruption of sun, moon, and stars will signal the utter destruction of the Temple itself, just as Jesus has predicted above in verse 2.

Mark's Jesus predicts the catastrophe now in verses 24–25 in the supratemporal, cosmic terms familiar to readers of the eschatological texts of the prophets. This is because the profundity of the Temple's devastation to the reigning religious powers will be such that only the symbolism of a cosmic cataclysm can express it. In these verses Jesus is loosely citing the Greek version of Isa 13:10 and 34:4, texts in which God's judgment on the nations, "the Day of the Lord," is stated in standard and familiar OT cosmic signs in the Septuagint:

> For the stars of heaven and Orion and all the heavenly firmament will not give light, and when *the sun* rises it *will be dark, and the moon will not give its light.* (Isa 13:10, LXX)

> And *all the powers of heaven* shall dissolve and heaven will be rolled up like a scroll, and all *the stars shall fall* like leaves from a vine and as leaves fall from a fig tree. (Isa 34:4, LXX)

Several observations about the rich meaning of these verses are necessary because of their apocalyptic language. First of all, in prophetic texts, and especially in Jewish apocalyptic writings, special cosmic metaphors are used to connote transcendent realms of good and of evil beyond the control of humans. The sun and moon represent the power of the false gods of the pagan world in such texts, and the stars are the focus of their idolatrous worship.[18] When the celestial power of these gods loses visibility, it is proof that the earthly powers they legitimate have been vanquished by God. They will fall one by one and be completely crushed, as, for example, when God says to the prophet, "I will shake the heavens and the earth; / I will overthrow the thrones of kingdoms" (Hag 2:21–22; cf. Amos 5:20; 8:9; Ezek 32:7; Joel 2:10).

Mark's Jesus has deliberately reused these OT symbolic texts to describe the destruction of the Jerusalem Temple as an illegitimate, idolatrous power, perfectly in keeping with his prophetic demonstration that it is no longer God's "house of prayer" (11:17). Furthermore, by using this symbolic language of the "Day of the Lord" he announces that the eschatological annihilation of every evil will start with the destruction of the Temple. It was the power center of the regime whose leaders will have been responsible for the death of Jesus and who have inflicted so much suffering on the people of Israel. This is foreshadowed by the cosmic reaction that "darkness came over the whole land" at the crucifixion of Jesus in 15:33, the only other mention of darkness in Mark.

The symbolic picture is completed at Jesus' death (a few verses later in 15:38), with the apocalyptic splitting of the Temple veil, the curtain separating the innermost sanctuary from the outer courts. This act of God nullifies the veil's symbolism as separating the Temple as the holy abode of God from all that is unholy, and thus forebodes its final destruction as useless in God's plan.

Second, exegetes often misunderstand Mark here, thinking that such eschatological judgment signals the end of our space-time continuum in some cosmic catastrophe, but this is not our Evangelist's intention. Only an overly literal interpretation of these apocalyptic texts can lead to this conclusion. If we look at the question critically, we find that none of the parallel texts in the Old Testament announce such a fate of the world. In fact, in almost all such texts, prophetic eschatology shows that life continues after such a visitation by God. Life then is actually better than ever, because it has been cleansed of evil by God. Just look at the conclusions to the prophetic texts Jesus cites in verses 24–25:

> When the LORD has pity on Jacob and again chooses Israel
> and settles them on their own soil. . . . (Isa 14:1)

> The desert and the parched land will exult; / the steppe will
> rejoice and bloom. / . . . / They will see the glory of the LORD, /
> the splendor of our God. (Isa 35:1–2)[19]

Third, another common mistake is to think that Mark believes that the events of 70 C.E., the destruction of Jerusalem and its Temple, indicate an imminent "End." The final Coming of the Lord is not temporally tied to the fate of the Temple, because Jesus has said in verse 10 that "the gospel must first be preached to all nations." That has not happened even to this day! The emphasis on the unparalleled strife in verse 20 indeed shows that the Temple's demise *was* a pivotal point in human history, but that is because the way is now open for the Kingdom of God to blossom as the true house of prayer, as Mark will point out in the last section of the Discourse (vv. 28–37).

Fourth, as I have pointed out in my introduction to apocalyptic symbolism, the polyvalence of apocalyptic language is designed to refer to a variety of events. Thus the cosmic cataclysm predicted here in verses 24–25 *also* refers to verses 7–8 in the first section of the Discourse, the inevitability of wars and insurrections *after* the devastation of Jerusalem. There Jesus has declared that many catastrophes "must happen, but it will not yet be the end" (v. 7). I believe that Mark used the mythical language of apocalyptic in verses 24–25 to apply to the destruction of the Temple. However, its poetic nature embraces any such divine destruction of the evil powers that oppress humankind, especially those that continue to cause the trial and execution of Christian preachers (vv. 9–13).[20] Since no temporal limits are set on these images of devastation, one cannot help but include the utter demise of totalitarian regimes in the middle and latter parts of the twentieth century!

Finally, Mark's Jesus has indeed spoken of the "End" in verse 7. He has clearly implied it in verse 10 and mentioned it again in verse 13. This "End" is the termination of the history of the world as we know it now, of its injustice and disharmony. Positively stated, the "End" is the full presence of the Kingdom of God, the *final* Coming of the Lord, a vision that permeated the apocalyptic eschatology of the early Church. Many modern interpreters think that it is this *final* Coming, the "End," that Mark refers to exclusively in the next two verses, but the Evangelist has something much more positive in mind!

Verse 26. At the conclusion of the OT text that Jesus has just cited, the prophet Isaiah predicted that after the fall of the oppressive powers (of Assyria and Edom), symbolized by the diminishment of their celestial sponsors, "*They will see the glory* of the LORD, / the splendor of our God" (Isa 35:2, cited above). This is one instance of many in which a great theophany, a "Day of the Lord," is predicted after the demise of evil. But here Mark says, "And *then they will see* 'the Son of Man coming in the clouds' with great power and glory." Jesus will proclaim to the Sanhedrin later in his trial before them, "*You will see* the Son of Man / seated at the right hand of the Power / and coming with the clouds of heaven" (14:62). Thus, for Mark, part of God's eschatological plan is that Jesus will come as the Son of Man on this "Day of the Lord," at the destruction of the Temple, the bastion of the Sanhedrin judiciary, but it will not be his final Coming.

Let's stop a moment and recall what we have learned about Jesus as "the Son of Man." The Son of Man is Jesus, who uses the title thirteen times of himself in Mark. Although the unusual title never provokes a reaction from a nonunderstanding public, the reader is left until now, in the Eschatological Discourse, for the full understanding of this enigmatic title, the full explanation of the "Messianic Secret."

The concept of the Son of Man is built on the vision scene in Daniel 7, where the prophet *saw* "a son of man [= "a human being" in the original Aramaic] *coming, / on the clouds* of heaven" who "received *dominion, glory, and kingship*" over all the nations" (Dan 7:13–14). The event is to happen in a renewed world after the disposal of the fourth beast (= the oppressive nation of the Syrian monarch Antiochus). In the Gospel of Mark, Jesus presents himself under the appellation of "*the* Son of Man" because of his deeds of "*power*" and because the "*Kingdom* of God" has drawn near in him. Here in 13:26 Mark's Jesus reveals that he will be seen "*coming* in the clouds with great *power* and *glory*" by the fallen powers of oppression, just as was predicted in the Book of Daniel.

Jesus presents himself as "the Son of Man" in Mark in four contexts: during his ministry, in anticipation of his suffering and death, as about to be manifested in his resurrection, and in his glorious return thereafter. However, Mark's understanding of time was culturally different from ours. He is definitely not thinking in our modern linear mode, as if there was a date set on some heavenly calendar for Jesus' glorious return. The Gospel envisions the power and glory of the Son of Man as already near throughout the ministry of Jesus, because that is his true identity in the heavenly sphere of God's truth.

At this point we are ready to delve more deeply into the symbolic thinking of our Evangelist and other first-century Christians. I have already discussed the ancient manner of imagining a celestial universe where the realities of the future on earth are already taking place. Since heaven is the divine sphere of reality, the images and revelations we receive from it are a way of understanding "thinking as God does" as a corrective to thinking "as human beings do" (8:33). This means that the *real truth* is what God wants, as opposed to merely human aspirations and the "necessary" conventions of ancient society. Rather than using abstract intellectual concepts to describe metaphysical reality (as we moderns might call the reality behind appearances), the ancients, symbolic thinkers that they were, used concrete figures and activities drawn on the celestial canvas of the imagination to disclose the hoped-for reality behind appearances.

This thinking is in the background when Mark presents Jesus' self-disclosure to the disciples in the heavenly glory of his Transfiguration (9:2–3). It is also meant to be perfectly clear to the High Priest and to the whole Sanhedrin at Jesus' trial when he predicts that he will fulfill the prophecy of Daniel, when they "will see the Son of Man / seated at the right hand of the Power / and coming with the clouds of heaven" (14:62). "Clouds" are a frequent symbol in the Old Testament for the presence of God[21] and are found in Mark only at the Transfiguration (9:7), here, when Jesus predicts his glorious return in 13:26, and at his trial before the

Sanhedrin (14:62). The *power* in which the Son of Man will come is divine *"power"* (cf. "the power of God" in 12:24 and the title of God as "Power" in 14:62), and true *"glory"* in the Bible is always that of God. Jesus has already spoken to his disciples of "the Son of Man . . . when he comes in his Father's glory," who will hold in shame those who are "ashamed of me and of my words in this faithless and sinful generation" (8:38). The members of the Sanhedrin are perfect candidates for this prediction.

The fact is that Jesus appears again and again at the tribulation of his "elect." As Mark's audience probably had heard, he came to Paul to end that zealot's terrible persecution of Christians (Acts 9:1–5). His appearance to Stephen, too, must have been well known, when he strengthened the saint at his martyrdom (Acts 7:56: "Behold, I see the heavens opened and the Son of Man standing at the right hand of God"). Furthermore, Paul says that "he appeared to more than five hundred brothers at once" (1 Cor 15:6). As Jesus has said to the Pharisees (8:2) and to his disciples (above in vv. 21–22), the Son of Man does not come with any preliminary signs or wonders. Just as the Holy Spirit will be present at any persecution of Christians (v. 11), so Jesus as the powerful Son of Man arrives on the scene (v. 26), at the downfall of any oppressive force that attempts to frustrate God's plan, to gather up the faithful into community. Humans never know when this will happen, but they have seen it again and again in history.

Verse 27. Mark's timeline here is very convincing: it was "after that tribulation" (v. 24) (= the siege of Jerusalem) that the cosmic portents in verses 24–25 would signal the demise of the Temple. Only "then," after that event, would the oppressive rulers see the power and glory of the Son of Man burst forth in a new house of prayer for all the nations, the success of the Christian mission. It is at a still later point in time, "and then" that he will "gather [his] elect from the four winds," again in a rereading of Isaiah 34–35: "For the mouth of the LORD has ordered it, / and his spirit shall gather them there" (34:16); "With divine recompense / [God] comes to save you" (35:4). The idea that God will gather the elect who are scattered throughout the earth, "from the four winds" (e.g., Zech 2:10) is common enough in the Old Testament, and points to God's gathering the people close to God's loving presence and the restoration of their rightful inheritance of peace and harmony. Here Jesus predicts that it will be he, as the Son of Man, who will come in divine power to fulfill the OT promise.

By the seemingly redundant addition here in verse 27, "from the end of the earth to the end of the sky," Mark begins to look forward to the final coming of the Son of Man, when the "elect" of Jesus will be made up of peoples from *all* the nations of the world. He envisions a great and diverse group when his disciples will have carried out their obligation that "the gospel . . .

be preached to all nations" (v. 10). They will be the "elect" people who have suffered much tribulation (v. 20) because of their steadfastness, and who will never be misled by false messiahs who perform the signs and wonders (v. 22) of impotent religious or political power. This great mission will commence after his resurrection when the Kingdom of God that Jesus predicted would "come in power" (9:1). And so what they will be gathered for is the final coming of the Son of Man, at the "End" (13:7, 13). Only after the success of that mission will he constitute the definitive humanity, the fulfillment of God's eternal plan for men and women.

Part 3 of the Discourse

We now come to the final double segment of the Discourse, a second overlay in which the material of its first two parts is further and finally explained. This third part will also answer the disciples' *double* question about the Temple and about the future "when all these things are about to come to an end" (v. 4). It is here that Jesus will show how the Son of Man comes again and again, after the destruction of the Temple, in the lives of the persecuted and otherwise tempted followers, until finally comes the end, the Parousia so important in the early Church.

Mark's Jesus says all this in part 3 of the Discourse, paradoxically, by means of two parables. First, he describes all that will happen in "this generation" (section *a*; v. 30). Then (section *b*; v. 32) he describes the return of the Lord again and again in the life of the Church until his final coming on "that day."

THE RIDDLE OF THE FIG TREE (VERSES 28–32)

Verses 28–30. Instead of the sign the disciples asked for in verse 4, Jesus gives them a parable/riddle in verse 28 about a fig tree becoming green and leafy. The problem is to figure out what the riddle means. Like a careful artist applying layer upon layer of pigment to build up the final effect in a painting, Mark's Jesus builds up his explanation of the parable in this and the next two verses.

"Learn a lesson from the fig tree" (v. 28a). The only other mention of a fig tree in the Gospel of Mark is the cursing and withering up of the leafy, green fig tree (11:13–14, 20–21), in a scene intercalated with Jesus' condemnation of the Temple (11:15–19). Scholars have long understood that Mark juxtaposed the two scenes in order to show in symbolic fashion Jesus' judgment on the worthlessness of the Temple. Because of this, the image of a fig tree in 13:28 first brings to the reader's mind the Temple, so forcefully condemned to destruction by Jesus in the introduction (v. 2) of this Discourse.

Mark reinforces the fig tree's allusion to the Temple in the next verse (v. 29) by repeating the words "*When you see* [these things happening]" that

Jesus used in verse 14 to allude to the Temple's desecration in the Book of Daniel: "When you see the desolating abomination." This repetition of "when you see" surely ties in with the use of the same verb in verse 26: "And then they [the oppressive powers] *will see* the Son of Man." Moreover, the phrase "*these things* (happening)" here repeats the phrase "these things" in the first part of the disciples' question in verse 4, which we have seen also refers to the destruction of the Temple. With all this attention on the Temple in this Discourse, ancient readers could not help but say, "Aha, that's the Temple!" when they heard Jesus say, "From the fig tree learn the lesson."

On a deeper level of symbolism Mark knows that the image of a fig tree is used in the eschatological scene of Isa 34:4 (LXX), "the stars shall fall like leaves from a vine and as leaves fall from a fig tree." But this is a continuation of the very text Jesus has just cited in verse 25 to present in cosmic terms the destruction of the Temple (see above). In the Old Testament the annihilation of oppressive political power is often symbolized by the disruption of the celestial powers of sun, moon, and stars. Jesus says in verse 29 that the appearance of "these things happening" signals that *something* (it is unnamed) "is near, at the gates." The unnamed *something* certainly refers to the coming of the Son of Man described in verses 26–27. Thus with the multivalent symbolism of the fig tree, Mark allows his community (and us) to see the destruction of the Temple in its proper eschatological perspective. As Jesus predicts, it is an important instance of the overthrow of oppressive power after which the glorious Son of Man will appear, but he remains "near, at the gates," poised at the ready to gather and heal his followers at the fall of other oppressive powers.

But there is much more to the symbol of the fig tree. In addition to Mark's careful allusion to the events mentioned previously in the Discourse, this canny author looks ahead to its final part. "When its branch becomes tender and sprouts leaves, you know that summer is near" (v. 28b). The *greening* of the fig tree, one of the few deciduous trees in ancient Palestine, is often taken by biblical commentators to refer to the suddenness of the onset of summer, and thus to connote the rapidity with which eschatological events take place. In fact, the suddenness of the coming of the Lord is underscored at the end of the Discourse by the parable of the sudden Return of the Master in verses 33–36. More immediately, however, the greening of the fig tree proposes a reversal of the *withering* of the fig tree in chapter 11, the symbol of the withering death of the Temple.

The image points to a *reblossoming* of God's elect in a summertime of new growth. Now the fig tree does not symbolize the worldly powerful Jerusalem Temple, but a new "house" of God, whose impact will not be from its great size and ornate buildings. Scholars agree that Mark considers the community of disciples of Jesus to be the new house of God, replacing the

Temple as "a house of prayer for all peoples" (11:17), and its cornerstone will be Jesus Christ himself (12:10).[22] Jesus will go on to describe this household in the final section of the Discourse. The blossoming of this house of God will always occur after the tribulations of Christian believers, which Jesus has predicted in the first part of this Discourse, together with the ravages of war that he calls "the birth pangs," sure signs of hope and new life. He will always be "near, at the gates" (v. 29).

In verse 30 Jesus affirms that "this generation will not pass away" until the occurrence of "*all* these things." In this statement Jesus includes all that is spoken about in the Discourse, namely, that within "this [Mark's] generation" the Son of Man will be present at all the deception and tribulation connected with the siege of the Temple. This includes the persecution and troubles of Christians mentioned in verses 9–13 and 14–20 and the destruction itself of the Temple, with its cosmic upheaval in verses 24–25. Finally, "*all* these things" refers to the wars to come with the devastation of the pagan powers (vv. 7–8), the Coming of the Son of Man (vv. 26–27), *and* the flourishing of the new Christian community, the new "house" of the Lord. Since Mark links up all these events by the repetition of the verb "to see," we can understand that the destruction of the Temple, indeed an event which will have taken place before "this generation will pass . . . away" (v. 30), is one instance of the overthrow of oppressive power in which the glorious Son of Man will have appeared. But there will be many more!

Confirmation of this interpretation is seen in the word of Jesus in 9:1, "There are some standing here who will not taste death until *they see* that the kingdom of God has come in power." For Mark the Son of Man has brought the Kingdom *in power* already in his readers' lifetime, namely, in the resurrection of Jesus (9:9). This leads to the historical regathering of the disciples "in Galilee" to preach the gospel. When Jesus quotes Dan 7:13 in verse 26, "And then they will see 'the Son of Man coming in the clouds' *with great power* and glory," Mark adds the word "power," which is not in the text of Daniel. Indeed, the Kingdom of God will come *in power* with the resurrected Jesus present in the establishment of the "household" of his disciples, "in this present age: houses and brothers and sisters and mothers and children" (10:30).

Jesus' *final* coming, "the End," can only be after "the gospel [is] preached to all nations" (13:10), an accomplishment yet to be carried out. Thus for Mark, Jesus, as the Son of Man, "comes" in every instance of Christian preaching and in their every moment of resolve to be faithful in tribulation, when the words of the Holy Spirit will be given to them in their "hour" (v. 11). Even when the oppression of war and persecution seems invincible, believers can remain faithful to the Christian mission to preach the gospel, because in it the Son of Man is present as surely as the greening of the fig tree portends the arrival of summer.[23] By this Discourse Jesus guarantees for Christians with divine authority that God's plan, the power of the Holy Spirit, and the powerful presence of the Son of Man are features of their mission. Thus they may have full confidence in the final victory of God's salvation, the world-wide process in which all earthly powers that oppress human beings will be overturned. Jesus has said, "I have told it all to you beforehand" (v. 23), and in the next verse he makes an even stronger guarantee.

Verse 31. "Heaven and earth will pass away, but my words will not pass away." For emphasis Jesus uses the literary device of hyperbole, a typical exaggeration common in Jewish rhetoric (compare Jesus' words in the Sermon on the Mount in Matt 5:18: "Amen, I say to you, until heaven and earth pass away"). We have seen that it is never said in the Bible that the earth will be completely destroyed, and how could heaven, the abode of God, ever pass away? No, this statement means that even if the impossible could happen, his promise will be upheld. "This generation" will see the destruc-tion of many apparently permanent things, but Jesus' words will never lose validity. They are in fact proved again and again by the collapse of the "inde-structible" in history.

Verse 32. In this statement the "day" is the Old Testament "Day of the Lord," the public manifestation of God's powerful salvation, but the "hour" is the critical moment of trial, just like the "hour" of Jesus' sufferings in 14:35 and 41. No one can predict the woes of one's personal future any more than the final history of the world, which is known only to God. Mark's answer to apocalyptic agitation is that "of that day or hour no one knows," because only God can bring about the "End" of injustice and strife in the world. In the imaginative future, "the day" of final salvation, the fulfillment of God's plan, will occur after the steadfastness of Christian preaching "the gospel to all nations" (v. 10), and their confidence to speak whatever is given "in that hour" by "the Holy Spirit" (v. 11).

Mark uses special language here when Jesus calls God "the Father" and himself "the Son." He reminds us of the love proclaimed by God's voice from heaven after the descent of the Spirit upon him in 1:11: "You are my *beloved* Son."[24] Even though the final history of the world is known only to God, you do not need to know the time if you are in the hands of such a loving Father.[25]

WATCHFULNESS FOR THE *KAIROS* (VERSES 33–37)

Verse 33. In this subsection the introductory imperative is doubled ("Be watchful! Be alert!"), and another apparent redundancy ("You do not know," repeating "no one knows" in the previous verse) tells us that Mark is empha-sizing again. The most important point of the whole discourse is that vigi-lance is necessary because no apocalyptic impostor can bring about or ever predict the *kairos* of the Lord's Coming. But history has another way of dulling the sharp blade of Christian preaching and working for justice.

Verse 34. Jesus explains this danger in another parable rich with allusion. The man going on a journey reminds us of the parable of the "man [who] planted a vineyard . . . and left on a journey," whose son was killed (12:1–9). As we have seen above in our discussion of Jesus' parables, the owner and the vineyard are God and God's Chosen People. When his son is killed, the owner gives the "vineyard" into the keeping of others, the nascent Church. In the present parable, however, Jesus is the "man" who "leaves his house," the symbol that represents the community of disciples.[26]

The Man gives *exousia* (elsewhere in Mark always the personal power/ authority of Jesus)[27] to his "servants" ("whoever wishes to be first among you [the disciples] will be the slave of all"; 10:44), just as Jesus sent forth the Twelve to preach and to have *exousia* to cast out demons in 3:14–15 (cf. 6:7). Each servant has his/her "work," a word that appears only one other time in Mark, the good "work" done by the woman with the alabaster jar in 14:6, and whose story will be told "wherever the *gospel is proclaimed* to the whole world" (14:9). Thus in this parable Jesus advises that each disciple has a specific and personal task, just as he has taught, to "deny [oneself], take up [one's] cross, and follow me" (8:34) in preaching the gospel "to all nations" (13:10).

The "gatekeeper" should not be understood as any specific Christian, for example, the apostles or other leaders of the Church, as in some commentaries. The command given to him/her "to watch" is exactly the same given to the Four in verse 35 and to "all" in verse 37. Rather, the "gatekeeper" should be understood as a clarification, another overlay of "servant." Thus all of Jesus' "servants" are "gatekeepers" who must be on watch because the Son of Man is "at the gates" (v. 29). The gatekeepers' task is not only to watch for the master's arrival, but to open the entrance to his (= the Son of Man's) house for all who would hear the preaching of the gospel.

Verse 35. Again the call to alertness, but this time it is "Watch!" (repeated "to all" in v. 37). We are admonished that the time of the Coming is unknown (vv. 32, 33) for a third time. Marcan redundancy? Look closely: Mark is reminding us that our "hour" (13:11, 32) will be like that of Jesus in Gethsemane, where he admonishes the disciples twice, with the same word, "Watch!" (14:34, 38). The four watches of the night, each spelled out here, anticipate moments in the Passion of Jesus in which the disciples fail to remain alert and to stand by their master.[28]

Verse 36. The words "[lest he] come . . . and find you sleeping" remind us of the behavior of Peter, James, and John, again, at the "hour" of Jesus in Gethsemane, "when he returned he found them asleep" (14:37, *repeated* in 40). Christians need to "Watch!" lest they repeat the sleepy behavior of the disciples at the "hour" of Jesus. They must give up all calculations about the End time and be awake during the obscurity of history, not becoming like those who receive the word and lose it by "tribulation or persecution . . . worldly anxiety, the lure of riches" (4:17, 19), which dull one into a false sense of security and well-being. If their mission is neglected, the gathering of the elect will be frustrated and delayed.[29]

Verse 37. Finally, we are not at all surprised when Jesus says, "What I say to you, [and stepping through the proscenium of the Gospel stage he says to us in the audience] I say to all." We have been applying his words to our present situation all along! All of history reposes in the sovereignty of God and thus the teaching of Jesus on the meaning of history is for all humanity.

SUMMARY

Reading Mark's thirteenth chapter carefully with the help of the perspectives outlined above in our introduction, and as embodied in recent Latin American exegesis, allows for a fuller understanding of the direction of the Discourse as well as the eschatological assertions of Jesus about the unfolding of God's plan for the future. Just as the artist Tiepolo devised his magnificent ceiling fresco to unfold an allegory as the viewer ascends the grand staircase in the magnificent Würzburg Residenz, so Mark has constructed the Eschatological Discourse. As readers move from level to level, they gain an ever fuller revelation of the ultimate reality Jesus promises to all.

Mark's community is concerned about the (forthcoming?) destruction of Jerusalem and its Temple, the symbolic center of the established religious leadership of Jesus' time. In the Discourse's introduction, Mark's Jesus, with divine authority, condemns the Temple to total destruction. The disciples misunderstand and think that Jesus is talking about an apocalyptic process of a full restoration of Israel and its Temple regime to world power. They put to him a double question about the fate of the Temple ("these things") and then about the final plan of God "when all these things are about to come to an end" (v. 4)

Jesus responds with a long Discourse, whose three sections are like overlays of the same material in each of which he responds to the disciples' first question about the destruction of the Temple. Then, instead of giving a time and full description of the End, he goes on to instruct them (each subsection b) on the interim after his death until his final Coming as the Son of Man, exhorting them to be vigilant and persevere until the End (vv. 13, 27, and 36).

In the first section of the Discourse (vv. 5–13) Jesus instructs the disciples (and later Christians) never to be tempted by anyone coming in his, the true Messiah's, name. This, as he will explain later in the second section, is because there will be no mistaking the return of Jesus as the glorious Son of Man. But here Jesus points out that the demise of Jerusalem cannot be the End because other more grandiose wars must follow the Jewish War. The true End that God has in mind can come about only through the painful process of a new birth for the whole world. That process requires the preaching of the gospel to all nations, an ongoing course of action in which many Christians will be persecuted. These faithful Christians will not suffer alone, however, since the Holy Spirit will be with them and tell them what to say. What they say will be the witness to God's plan, the gospel, and faithfulness to it to the End (of one's life and of the evangelization of the whole world) will guarantee salvation, because God will bring it about through the Christian mission.

Mark returns in a second section (vv. 14–23) to the question of the Jerusalem Temple and the Jewish War, which may have still been going on at the time of Mark's writing. The proper response of Christians in Judea is to flee the city with full reliance on God's mercy. The Temple and all its religious system must be destroyed, but this is only one example of the coming demise of oppressive religiopolitical systems. Many more must tumble before all of humanity can live a free and fully human life. Any would-be Messiah at this time is an impostor, no matter how deceptive his power, because Jesus has already told us beforehand that there is much to come after the destruction of Jerusalem. The very imperial power of Rome, and any other oppressive power, will be eclipsed by the divine power and glory of Jesus who comes as the Son of Man. His final task is to gather into a new community the faithful of all nations who believe in the gospel.

In a third section (vv. 28–37) Mark uses the riddle of the Fig Tree to show that this coming of Jesus in power and glory happens suddenly, as in the destruction of the Temple regime and its heartless exploitation in Mark's present time ("this generation"). Many such seemingly indestructible oppressors will likewise pass away, but, as Jesus assures us at the end of each subsection, all follows the plan of God.

No one but God can know the exact time of Christian tribulation ("the hour") or of the Day of the Lord ("the day" of final salvation), but Jesus can guarantee that all will occur in due season. Jesus will go away in the resurrection, like the Man Who Went Abroad (v. 34), and leave behind his faithful followers endowed with his *exousia* as gatekeepers to welcome all nations into the new covenant community. Each suffering ("hour") of a Christian is a *kairos* in which the gospel can be witnessed and preached, and in which the divine power and glory of Jesus can manifest itself and diminish the sovereignty of all oppressors. This requires the attentiveness admonished in all the many imperatives throughout the Discourse, so that *every* Christian uses Jesus' *exousia*. It was given to the very first disciples, but is now given to all (v. 37), each according to his or her work, to preach and witness with the Holy Spirit to the truth of the gospel. Thus Jesus invites us to conversion and a new life of concern for the salvation of others.[30] The Christian as "gatekeeper" is on watch, for the Son of Man is "at the gates," forthcoming and energizing every situation.[31] Because of Jesus' guarantee, daily life ("experienced time") can now be united to eternal life ("imagination time"). Jesus is the "Lord" of each step along the way of life. He may return at any one of them.[32]

As for the final coming of the Son of Man, exactly when this will occur is unknown as ensconced in God's future, but, according to Mark, it can only happen when the Christian message of love and equality spreads throughout the whole world. Just as its timing is unknown to us, so its exact nature remains a mystery in God's plan.

NOTES

1. Notice how imperative verbs completely define the Discourse and give it a driving force: "See, watch" (vv. 5, 9), "Do not be alarmed" (v. 7), "Do not worry" (v. 11), "[they] must flee" (v. 14), "Pray" (v. 18), "Do not believe it" (v. 21), "Learn" (v. 28), "Know" (v. 29), Be alert" (v. 33), "Be watchful" (vv. 23, 33, cf. 37).

2. This Marcan technique is explored by Mateos and Camacho in their excellent study *Evangelio, figuras y símbolos* (2nd ed.; Córdoba, Spain: El Almendro, 1992). Mark's repetitive style has been more fully explored by Paul Danove in "The Rhetoric of the Characterization of Jesus as the Son of Man and Christ in Mark," *Biblica* 84 (2003): 16–34, esp. 19–20.

3. Collins, *The Apocalyptic Imagination: An Introduction to Jewish Apocalyptic Literature* (2nd ed.; Grand Rapids: Eerdmans, 1998), 107–8.

4. Kealy, *The Apocalypse of John* (Message of Biblical Spirituality 15; Collegeville, Minn.: Liturgical Press, 1990), 127; cf. 193.

5. Jesus is shown as "seated" only four times in Mark. Here and in 4:1 he sits to teach, but in 12:36 and 14:62 he sits "at [God's] right hand [of power]." A mountain is stereotypically a place of divine authority or encounter in the Bible (as it is previously in Mark 3:13; 6:46; 9:2, 9).

6. Luke produces a similar effect when he takes over this discourse of Mark. He omits the words, "And it is necessary that the gospel *be preached to all nations*," from Mark 13:10 in his parallel apocalyptic discourse in Luke 21. Rather, he has the glorified Jesus say these words after he has been raised from the dead: "it is written . . . that repentance, for the forgiveness of sins (= the gospel of Jesus for Luke!), would *be preached* in his name *to all nations* (Luke 24:46–47).

7. This striking symbolism has been observed both by Mateos and Camacho (*Evangelio, figuras y símbolos,* 197) and G. Cook and R. Foulkes (*Marcos: Comentario bíblico hispano-americano* [Miami: Caribe, 1993], 339).

8. The verb form "it is necessary" refers to God's will for the participation of humans in God's eschatological plan in all its uses in Mark: in 8:31 Jesus must suffer; in 9:11 John the Baptist has to fulfill Malachi's messianic prophecy of Elijah's return; in 14:31 Peter ironically predicts his suffering role in the future Church; and three times here in chap. 13 (vv. 7, 10, and negatively in 14) God's will is stated for the playing out of salvation history.

9. The same image of the "labor pains" of new birth is used by St. Paul in Rom 8:22, where Christians are to await "the glory to be revealed" (Rom 8:18).

10. Fritzleo Lentzen-Deis, *El Evangelio de San Marcos: modelo de nueva evangelización* (Santafé de Bogotá: Consejo Episcopal Latinoamericano, 1994), on Mark 13:10.

11. This powerful insight is from Mateos and Camacho, *Marcos,* 224.

12. G. Gorgulho and A. F. Anderson, *O Evangelho e a vida: Marcos* (3rd ed.; São Paulo: Paulinas, 1978), 47.

13. The words are from Juan Mateos, *Marcos 13: El grupo cristiano en la historia* (Lectura del Nuevo Testamento 3; Madrid: Cristianidad, 1987), 476, but Cook and Foulkes (*Marcos,* 352) and José Maria González Ruiz (*Evangelio según Marcos: Introducción, traducción, comentario* [Estella, Spain: Verbo Divino, 1988], 198) are of exactly the same mind.

14. Collins, *Apocalptic Imagination,* 51.

15. In fact, Caligula's proposal of 44 C.E. was never carried out, and by the time of the siege of Jerusalem itself in 70 C.E., it would have been impossible (and fatal) to follow the directive of flight in v. 15. The Roman *circumvallatio* (siegeworks) that surrounded the city by that time was inescapable.

16. This interpretation of Cook and Foulkes (345) shows the facility with which Latin Americans understand the symbolic nature of the images in biblical narrative.

17. At least two revolutionary leaders in the Jewish War are candidates for Mark's fear of false Messiahs, Menachem bar Jehuda and Simon bar Giora (both mentioned in Josephus' *Jewish War,* 2.17 and 22); among modern false Messiahs one thinks immediately of Jim Jones of Jonestown and David Koresh of the Branch Davidian movement.

18. Very similar in the cosmic imagery of the sun and moon are the following OT texts: Isa 24:19, 21; Jer 4:23; Ezek 32:7–8; Joel 2:10; 3:4; 4:15; Amos 8:9, and these later Jewish apocalyptic texts: *1 Enoch* 80:4–7; *4 Ezra* 7:39; cf. the Christian *Apocalypse of Peter* 5; Rev 8:12; 9:2. The connection of the stars with idolatry may be seen in Deut 4:19; 17:3; Jer 8:2; Ezek 8:16; *2 Esdras* 5:4 and the *Sybilline* Oracles 5.155–57; cf. Rev 6:13.

19. See also the conclusions to the other texts we have cited: Isa 25:3–4; Jer 5:18; Ezek 36:8–11; Joel 3:5; Amos 9:8–9.

20. Collins puts it this way: "apocalypses . . . share the poetic nature of myth and allude symbolically to a fullness of meaning that can never be reduced to literalness" (*Apocalyptic Imagination,* 108).

21. A good example is the Pillar of Cloud in Exodus chaps. 13–14 which is seen as the presence of God with the people as they wander through the desert; see also Exod 19:16; 40:38; Ezek 38:9, 16; Ps 68:34; 89:7; cf. Acts 1:9.

22. See the excellent discussion of the Christian community as a new "house" of prayer replacing the Temple by Sharyn Dowd (*Prayer, Power, and the Problem of Suffering: Mark 11:22–25 in the Context of Markan Theology* [SBLDS 105; Atlanta: Scholars Press, 1988], 52–55. Susan R. Garrett (*The Temptations of Jesus in Mark's Gospel* [Grand Rapids: Eerdmans, 1998], 119–24 and 163–69) cites Dowd and expands her explanation to include the kind of prayer needed in God's new Temple. For a concise and classic statement of this theology see R. E. Brown, *The Death of the Messiah* (ABRL; New York: Doubleday, 1994), 1:453; also D. H. Juel, *Messiah and Temple: The Trial of Jesus in the Gospel of Mark* (Missoula, Mont.: Scholars Press, 1977), 157.

23. "The Gospel makes Jesus present in the act of preaching, and his 'secret' [his saving death and resurrection] is penetrated more and more deeply by those who believe in him." So Ana Flora Anderson in a kind clarification for me of statements in G. Gorgulho and A. F. Anderson, *O Evangelho e a vida: Marcos* (São Paulo: Paulinas, 1978), 15–16.

24. Mateos, *Marcos 13,* 408. Similar words are said by God: "This is my beloved Son," at the Transfiguration (9:7), the first indication of Jesus' glory.

25. González Ruiz, *Evangelio según Marcos,* 200.

26. The "house" of the disciples of Jesus is mentioned often in the Gospel (1:29; 2:15; 9:33; 10:10; 14:3). As we have pointed out above, the Church is the "new house of prayer for all the peoples" (11:17).

27. *Exousia* is used eight other times in Mark: the *exousia* of Jesus' teaching in 1:22 and 27, that of the Son of Man to forgive sins in 2:10, the *exousia* Jesus gives his disciples to drive out demons in 3:15 and 6:7, and in the question by the chief priests, scribes and elders about Jesus' *exousia* to condemn the Temple in 11:28, 29, 33.

28. "Evening" occurs again in 14:17 at the Last Supper, when Jesus predicts the betrayal by Judas and the denial of Peter. "Midnight" is about the time that the inner circle of Jesus' disciples fell asleep at Jesus' agony in Gethsemane, his betrayal by Judas, and the flight of all the disciples at his arrest. "Cockcrow" is the moment of Peter's denial in 14:72, and "in the morning" is when the Sanhedrin hands Jesus over to Pilate for the sentence of death (15:1; cf. "morning" at the flight of the women at the tomb in 16:2).

29. Mateos and Camacho, *Marcos,* 236.

30. Paulo Evaristo Cardinal Arns, *O evangelho de Marcos* (2nd ed.; São Paulo: Paulus, 1997), 121.

31. G. Gorgulho and A. F. Anderson, *A justiça dos pobres: Mateus* (2nd ed.; São Paulo: Ed. Paulinus, 1981), 223.

32. Lentzen-Deis, *El Evangelio de San Marcos,* on Mark 13:35.

CONCLUSIONS ON
THE KINGDOM TO COME IN MARK

As has been evident all along the way, our study of the Gospel of Mark has an important theological motive. The task we set for ourselves was to employ the very best exegesis of the Gospel of Mark, especially the excellent insights of Latin American scholars, in an interpretation of Jesus' great eschatological promise, the Kingdom of God. We have acknowledged that Mark and his first-century community belonged to an ancient, prescientific culture that perceived and expressed the truth about reality quite differently from our modern North Atlantic manner. We have attempted to enter more fully into their mindset by means of the cultural findings of social science criticism and the Latin American experience in order to break open the meaning of the sacred text for our lives today. But we must do more than this.

We and all the readers of Mark's Gospel are called to apply the meaning of Jesus' words to our own lives. If it is to be effective at all, the gospel of Jesus Christ must be realized in our world. The Kingdom of God does not come by theologizing or with even the best humanistic theory. Our study must result in "the formation of the Christian community, the social embodiment of the early Christian faith."[1]

We have examined how Mark identifies Jesus (Christology) as the Son of God and the Son of Man, the fulfillment of Daniel's prophecy, and much more than the expected Messiah. He is the perfection of weak humanity become strong in the power of God. He is the Son of God in his prayerful closeness and his selfless obedience to the Father. He is the Son of Man in his divine power over sin and the Law, in his special concern for the poor, in his atoning death and resurrection, and in every subsequent glorious coming to his followers.

What an awesome figure Mark presents as the Son of Man, the poor carpenter in whom the fullness of humanity is achieved in fidelity to God, his loving Father, and in whom humanity achieves its fullness! He is the one who can bridge the chasm between the true desire of God for our world and its present reality. He is the reality of God's dominion over us, and at the same time the symbol of all of us who do God's will in service of life over against the powers of death. What confidence he must have inspired in the early Church in the face of the persecutions of the mighty Roman Empire!

We have seen that Jesus' teaching on the Kingdom of God is an urgent message for today, but it has not always been vigorously pursued by Christians, who have often allowed its "functional displacement" by an individualistic appropriation of the quite orthodox doctrines of the presence of the Holy Spirit, the efficacy of the sacraments, and the belief in personal immortality.[2] We need to re-express Jesus' message for contemporary application in our lives, for our salvation and for that of the whole world.[3]

The Gospel of Mark has spoken of the future with an apocalyptic vision, in what we might call a "sky language," in which what is *really the truth* about humanity is described as already having become a reality in the divine sphere and just waiting to happen in the earthly one. Mark's insight is that we cannot just sit back and wait for God to destroy all evil in the world, but that God intends to bring about universal peace and justice in only one way. God has sent Jesus, perfect in his human nature, to show all the rest of us exactly what we must do so that God's power can triumph on earth.

If Jesus did not come down from the cross two thousand years ago to save himself and to force our belief in God's plan, why would he do so at some point in the future? As Mark the Evangelist points out, Jesus is not coming as the Son of Man in violence to reverse history, but to gather the elect into community whenever they turn to him to lead the way to the Father. Change will come about when people follow Jesus' way and give up on their own solution to the world's problems. There is no merely military or political solution to them!

Only God can bring about the solution, and God wants it to come about through the witness of those who believe in the gospel. They must follow Jesus' preaching of a new manner of living in love of all people with the decision to share all that they have. The truth is that the Son of Man does not yet reign fully on earth. He is beyond history, but not on the margin of history, constantly empowering his followers in the struggle to restore a human face on a world dominated by beasts, just as predicted in the Book of Daniel.[4]

In Mark's Eschatological Discourse, Jesus' repeated commands to "Watch!" and "Be vigilant" are calls to constant prayer for those who would follow him. To understand the vision of the Kingdom of God we need to do more than just study its symbolism. We need to have the same faith that Jesus had, and to practice discernment in prayer as he did throughout his ministry and in his agony in Gethsemane. Only in this way may we, too, discover God's will for us in every situation.[5]

I would like to tell a modern parable in which a spatial metaphor is used to shed light on the unique temporal nature of the Kingdom. A parable is a metaphor, a comparison of some concrete image to the abstract idea of the Kingdom of God. It is not to be taken literally any more than one ought to think that the Kingdom of God really is a mustard seed. By using some modern imagery perhaps we may come to an understanding of Jesus' ancient teaching, the announcement of what could be because it already is.

> The Kingdom of God is like an interglactic spacecraft (not unlike the starship *Enterprise* of *Star Trek* fame). For many centuries it has been in constant orbit around the earth, invisible, because of its "cloaking" device, and known only to those on earth who have believed in its power. The starship is populated by wonderful beings whose philosophy and technology are completely dedicated to the search for the good, and its tremendous power is available to all those who dedicate their lives to the betterment of human life everywhere. The "Prime Directive," however, of all those connected with the starship is that no *violent* intervention in earthly life is ever permitted, so that no human being, however evil, may ever be *coerced* to live humanly, for that is a contradiction.
>
> Once, when the nations of the earth were on the brink of war, someone thought it would be a good idea to immobilize the combatants harmlessly with some of the pharmaceuticals commonly used for medical treatment on the starship. This would cause a break in the fighting and provide much needed time for a diplomatic solution to the problem. The idea had to be abandoned, however, when it was realized that some earth scientists could analyze such a substance only to turn it into a new superweapon for their own purposes. Another well-meaning crew member suggested that people on earth be given the secret to the Star People's safe and totally reusable power source. But that idea

was abandoned when earth people confirmed that the technology would just be hoarded by the more advanced nations to enslave the rest of the world economically. The good members of the starship then realized that there was nothing they could do to deter the nations of the earth from violence. They could only teach peace and fraternity, and hope that the earthlings would figure out for themselves that war is never a solution.

In the Kingdom of God, what is right must be chosen freely, based on the knowledge that can be gained only by those who live with "human dignity for all" as their immediate goal. Following Jesus means to turn from an orientation to the Temple to an orientation to God's people. The leaders of the Kingdom never want to replace the tyranny of human political, economic, or religious power with their own suzerainty, but invite a collaborative effort of all who believe to form a future as yet unimagined. In it every human being will be treated with dignity even if he or she chooses to renounce it.[6] Merely giving money to the poor does not do the poor justice, for it does not incorporate them into community. We must make them more than the mere objects of our charity. Following the example of Jesus, we must welcome them into our midst with love and allow them to be fully humanized once more by sharing responsibility in the community, no matter how weak they may be at first.

The repentance and change of heart we need is to stop thinking of the world as beyond our help. We must stop living only for a reward in heaven and start caring for our human family, especially for those who are so dehumanized by hunger and ignorance that they cannot embrace a loving God. Prosperity for all is not an impossible matter, for when people share what they have, there is always enough. Indeed there always was enough, a hundredfold of what really matters to human existence, because your love can count a hundred times if you choose to share it.

What will come after all unjust systems are overthrown by the Holy Spirit's powerful witness in believers in the hopeful message of Jesus? The final Coming of the Son of Man will see the whole world gathered into communities of justice, for that is the eschatological horizon of human existence, the complete realization of the full potential of humanity. This is Jesus' urgent message for us today. What would the reign of the really just be like?[7]

NOTES

1. J. Nissen, "Jesus, the People of God, and the Poor: The Social Embodiment of Biblical Faith," in *New Directions in Biblical Theology* (ed. S. Pedersen; Leiden: Brill, 1994), 221.

2. David E. Aune, "The Significance of the Delay of the Parousia for Early Christianity," in *Current Issues in Biblical and Patristic Interpretation: Studies in Honor of Merrill C. Tenney* (ed. G. F. Hawthorne; Grand Rapids: Eerdmans, 1975), 107.

3. Pope John Paul II has voiced this Christian desire very clearly in the *Message of His Holiness Pope John Paul II for the Celebration of the World Day of Peace.* We can only reprint a small part of this seven-page document, which should be read in full:

> Is this not the time for all to *work together for a new constitutional organization of the human family,* truly capable of ensuring peace and harmony between peoples, as well as their integral development? . . . [This] means continuing and deepening processes already in place to meet the almost universal *demand for participatory ways of exercising political authority, even international political authority, for transparency and accountablity at every level of public life.*

Pacem in Terris: A Permanent Commitment (Jan. 1, 2003), online: http://www.vatican.va/holy_father/john_paul_ii/messages/peace/documents/hf_jp-ii_mes_20021217_xxxvi-world-day-for-peace_en.html.

4. José Maria González Ruiz, *Evangelio según Marcos: Introducción, traducción, comentario* (Estella: Verbo Divino, 1988), 44.

5. João Wenzel, *Pedagogia de Jesus segundo Marcos* (São Paulo: Ed. Paulinas, 1997), 163.

6. We must cultivate Jesus' divine trait of compassion for all our fellow human beings, as we see so clearly in the U.S. Conference of Catholic Bishops' powerful *Statement on Iraq:* "In assessing whether 'collateral damage' is proportionate, the lives of Iraqi men, women and children should be valued as we would the lives of members of our own family and citizens of our own country" (U.S.C.C.B., Nov. 13, 2002, online: http://www.usccb.org/bishops/iraq.htm).

7. Thanks to Fr. Johan Konings for this penetrating question, which came after a most delightful two days of study and conversation at the Jesuit Instituto Sant Inácio in Belo Horizonte, Brazil.

SELECT BIBLIOGRAPHY

Aguirre, Rafael. *La mesa compartida: Estudios del NT desde las ciencias sociales.* Presencia teológica 77. Santander, Spain: Sal Terrae, 1994.

Arns, Paulo Evaristo Cardinal. *O evangelho de Marcos.* 2nd ed. São Paulo: Paulus, 1997.

Balancin, Euclides. *Como ler o evangelho de Marcos: Quem é Jesus?* 3rd ed. São Paulo: Paulus, 1991.

Bravo, Carlos. *Jesús, hombre en conflicto: El relato de Marcos en América Latina.* 2nd ed. Mexico City: Centro de Reflexión Teológica, 1996.

Cárdenas Pallares, José. *Un pobre llamado Jesús.* Mexico City: Casa unida de publicaciones, 1982.

Cook, Guillermo, and Ricardo Foulkes. *Marcos: Comentario bíblico hispanoamericano.* Miami: Caribe, 1993.

de la Calle, Francisco. *A teologia de Marcos.* São Paulo: Ed. Paulinas, 1978.

González Ruiz, José Maria. *Evangelio según Marcos. Introducción, traducción, comentario.* Estella, Spain: Verbo Divino, 1988.

Gorgulho, Gilberto, and Ana Flora Anderson. *O evangelho e a vida: Marcos.* São Paulo: Paulinas, 1978.

Konings, Johan. *Marcos.* A Bíblia passo a passo. São Paulo: Loyola, 1994.

Lentzen-Deis, Fritzleo. *El evangelio de San Marcos: modelo de nueva evangelización.* Santafé de Bogotá: Consejo Episcopal Latinamericano, 1994.

Mateos, Juan. *Marcos 13: El grupo cristiano en la historia.* Lectura del Nuevo Testamento 3. Madrid: Cristianidad, 1987.

Mateos, Juan, and Fernando Camacho. *Evangelio, figuras y símbolos.* 2nd ed.; Córdoba, Spain: El Almendro, 1992.

———. *Marcos: Texto y Comentario.* Córdoba, Spain: El Almendro, 1994.

Mesters, Carlos. *Caminhamos ná estrada de Jesus: o evangelho de Marcos.* National Conference of Brazilian Bishops. São Paulo: Paulinas, 1996.

———. *Defenseless Flower: A New Reading of the Bible.* Maryknoll, N.Y.: Orbis, 1989.

———. *The Hope of the People Who Struggle: The Key to Reading the Apocalypse of St. John.* Athlone, South Africa: Theology Exchange Program, 1994.

Morales, Mardonio. *San Marcos.* Mexico City: Centro de Reflexión Teológica, 1998.

Mosconi, Luis. *Evangelho de Jesus Cristo segundo Marcos.* São Paulo: Loyola, 1997.

Pikaza, Xabier. *Pan, casa, palabra. La iglesia en Marcos.* Biblioteca de estudios bíblicos 94. Salamanca, Spain: Sigueme, 1998.

———. *Para vivir el evangelio. Lectura de Marcos.* Estella, Spain: Verbo Divino, 1995.

Susin, Xabier. *Assim na terra como no céu: Brevilóquio sobre Eschatologia e Criação.* Petropolis, Brazil: Vozes, 1995.

Wenzel, João Inácio. *Pedagogia de Jesus segundo Marcos.* São Paulo: Ed. Paulinas, 1997.

INDEX OF
BIBLICAL TEXTS

New Testament

INDEX OF
MODERN AUTHORS